The Novels of Ayi Kwei Armah

In the same series

Recent Commonwealth Literature (2 Vols.)
Ed. R.K. Dhawan, A.K. Srivastava and P.V. Dhamija

The Novels of Wole Soyinka
M. Rajeshwar

Indian Response to African Writing
Ed. A. Ramakrishna Rao and C.R. Visweswara Rao

South Asian Response to Chinua Achebe
Ed. Bernth Lindfors and Bala Kothandaraman

Australian Literature and Indian Literature: Studies in Mutual Response
Ed. David Kerr and R.K. Dhawan

Australian Literature Today
Ed. R.K. Dhawan and David Kerr

New Zealand Literature Today
Ed. R.K. Dhawan and Walter Tonetto

A.D. Hope: Questions of Poetic Strength
Walter Tonetto

THE NOVELS OF AYI KWEI ARMAH

K. Damodar Rao

Published by
Prestige Books
3/28, East Patel Nagar
New Delhi 110 008

ISBN: 81-85218-75-7

Phototypesetting by
Pivot Computers
Delhi 110 006
Ph. 291 8404

Printed at
Mehra Offset Press
New Delhi 110 002

Contents

Preface
7

Acknowledgements
9

The Way of Reciprocity
Introductory
11

The Waking of the Powerless
The Beautyful Ones Are Not Yet Born
33

In Search of Wholeness:
Fragments
55

Connecting Centre:
Why Are We So Blest?
74

Destruction of Destroyers
Two Thousand Seasons
89

The Beautiful Ones Are Born:
The Healers
108

Conclusion
121

Bibliography
128

Index
136

Preface

Ayi Kwei Armah, the brilliant Ghanaian novelist, is an articulate spokesman of African history and identity. Through a process of diagnosis/analysis of contemporary reality and reclamation/reconstruction of African history Armah, in his fictional medium, embarks on a course of restoration which at the same time serves as "an aggressive response to the colonialist theory of pre-colonial barbarism."[1] Frantz Fanon, the Martinican psychiatrist-revolutionary, while analysing the role of the native intellectual in the post-colonial context, formulates that the African creative writer in the process of evolutionary growth creates "a fighting literature, a revolutionary literature and a national literature" transforming himself into "an awakener of his people."[2] Armah's incisive probing into the matrix of Africa's past and present in an attempt to celebrate the principles of reciprocity and positive change points to such a fighting and national literature. His fictional creation is the summation of his sustained efforts to approach and dismantle colonial and neo-colonialist structures.

Since the publication of *The Beautyful Ones Are Not Yet Born* (1968) Armah has attracted critical attention by sheer excellence of his art. Initially, there were bitter voices that complained of his outsiderist posture and characterized him as a startling novelist, an "unpredictable enfant terrible at drastic odds with the literary establishment."[3] The proliferation of an appreciative body of Armah criticism is of fairly recent origin and that too is limited to analyses of individual novels. Sustained and concerted efforts to capture and present the contribution of Armah to the growth of the African fiction in English have been few and far between. The present study while taking into account the considerable body of criticism on Armah's art tries to synthesize the positive thrust of Armah's vision in the light of his fictional achievement. It presents him as a pioneer and a path-finder who has evolved a genuine poetics of the African novel. If the individual stance as an exemplification of communal experience in *The Beautyful Ones Are Not Yet Born* opened up exciting possibilities, the experimentation in theme, technique and structural rhythms as manifested in *Fragments* and *Why Are We So Blest?* signifies an evolving African aesthetic that is tantamount to a revolution in the field of fiction. But it is the daring exposition of the group consciousness in *Two Thousand Seasons* and *The Healers* employing history and folk-tale as theme and spontaneity, innovation and improvisation as technique and structure in the best tradition of the oral narrative structure that marked a break from all the received patterns of novel form.

Armah, in addition to being an experimentalist par excellence, is a great synthesizer. The perfect fusion of individual and communal welfare, national realities and Pan-African ideal, contemporary situation and historical vision is presented in medicative processes and therapeutic terms. All the novels of Armah – from *The Beautyful Ones Are Not Yet Born* through *The Healers* – provide a dialectic in this direction. The fusion of alternatives, the synthesis of corroboratives and the celebration of the preservable models of the past in any process of reconstruction define the psychological therapy resorted to by Armah in approaching neo-colonialist structures. In this respect, Armah's novels could be taken as a fictional statement on Fanon's formulations about the psychological implications of colonialism, neo-colonialism and violence. The present study attempts to analyse and examine, in the light of historicity, the dynamics of social change mediated in the novels of Armah. While tracing the two mutually dependent analytical/critical/national and historical/continental/constructive phases in Armah's fiction, the study attempts to elicit the integration achieved in thematic and structural polarities.

Parts of this book have appeared in literary journals: "Armah's *The Beautyful Ones Are Not Yet Born*: A Study in the Aesthetics of Negation" was published in *Kakatiya Journal of English Studies* (1990); "Decolonizing the Mind: A Dialectic of the Personal and the Continental in Ayi Kwei Armah's *Why Are We So Blest?*" in *Triveni* (Jan.-June, 1991); "Destruction of Destroyers: Thematic and Structural Polarities in Armah's *Two Thousand Seasons*" in *New Quest* (July-August, 1991); "Work of Masters in the Arts of Eloquence: *The Healers*" in *Kakatiya Journal of English Studies* (1991). I wish to record my deep sense of gratitude to the editors of these journals.

In writing this book, I have been benefited by the writings and insights of Lewis Nkosi, Chidi Amuta, Neil Lazarus and Robert Fraser. I wish to acknowledge my profound sense of gratitude to these critics.

NOTES

1. Frantz Fanon, *The Wretched of the Earth* (London: Penguin, 1967), p. 168.
2. *Ibid.*, p. 179.
3. Robert Fraser, *The Novels of Ayi Kwei Armah* (London: Heinemann), p. ix.

Acknowledgements

I wish to record my deep sense of gratitude to Dr. K. Indrasena Reddy who supervised the present project and taught me the nuances of research discipline; to Prof. S. Laxmana Murthy, Prof. P. Shiv Kumar, Prof. A. Jaganmohana Chari, Dr. P. Mallikarjuna Rao, Dr. T. Vinoda, Dr. M. Rajagopalachari, Dr. M. Rajeshwar and Mr. V. Srinivas for their help at different stages of my research; to Mr. S. Sadasiva, Mr. K. Satyanarayana, Dr. Ch. V. Purshotham Reddy and Mr. V. Krishna Rao for their help and advice; to Dr. R.K. Dhawan of Delhi University for his help and encouragement; to Dr. L. Ramaiah, Librarian, CIEFL, for making facilities at the institute available to me; to Dr. K. Jayashankar, Vice-Chancellor, and Prof. C.K. Kokate, Co-ordinating Officer, for providing me partial financial assistance for the publication of this study; to my wife Radha, and to my sons, Vinay and Vineel for their affection and inspiration which sustained me during the period of my research; to Mrs. D. Renu of Prestige Books for bringing out the book elegantly in a remarkably short period.

K. Damodar Rao

To the memory of my mother

The Way of Reciprocity: Introductory

Ayi Kwei Armah is one of the most controversial novelists that Anglophone Africa has produced to date. The controversy that surrounded him with the publication of his first novel, *The Beautyful Ones Are Not Yet Born* (1968) was compounded when he followed it with two more novels, *Fragments* (1970) and *Why Are We So Blest?* (1972). However, in his later works, *Two Thousand Seasons* (1973) and *The Healers* (1978), as the total consciousness of a whole people is sought to be unfolded, a true perspective of Armah's concerns becomes apparent.

Armah is often referred to as a pessimist and a cynic mostly because of his first three novels. These novels, in fact, belong to the analytical stage while *Two Thousand Seasons* and *The Healers* could be considered as belonging to the constructive phase. Part of the controversy that surrounds his earlier novels emanates from the deliberate stance of the novelist as an observer, an outsider and an alien. The critical response to Armah's fiction, to begin with, was unfavourable which later became pronounced with misplaced hostility. The Western critical opinion, in particular, patronisingly greeted Armah for portraying universal themes of alienation and degradation in all walks of Ghanaian life. But the scathing attack on the Arab/Islamic and Christian/European/Imperialist colonisers in *Two Thousand Seasons* prompted accusations of rabid communalism, anti-racial racism, in short, Negritude reborn. Since then, several attempts have been made to touch the core of the meaning carefully posited behind a complex symbolic structure in each of Armah's novels. His ability as a novelist is never disputed, but his fiction is seldom accorded its due acclaim.

African literature, specified by its context, is closely linked to its soil and society. A study of the three phases of African history—pre-colonialism, colonialism and post-colonialism—could be very helpful for the proper appraisal and evaluation of the works of any African writer. This appears to be all the more relevant in the case of Armah in whose works the overall view sometimes provides overlapping images and sometimes assumes the role of a central character. It also brings into light the dialectical relationship between the setting and action as also between content and form mediated in the novels of Armah. A close reading of the complex web of symbols and images into which he has carefully woven his fervent concern for the subjugated masses and also an encompassing historical vision shed light on the various factors that make him the most effective, articulate and a vehement spokesman of the history and values of the African people. In this respect, a study of his works and vision becomes a fascinating proposition. The polarization of critical opinion concerning Armah's brilliance adds a new dimension to the study.

Ayi Kwei Armah was born in 1939 at Takoradi, a harbour city in Western Ghana. He had his collegiate education at Achimota and later spent several years in America as a student and as a teacher. His return to Ghana in 1964 was marked by a deep sense of loss and disillusionment with the Ghanaian situation in the aftermath of independence.

The hypocrisy of nationalist leaders like Nkrumah and the simple act of stepping into the shoes of colonial masters prompted Armah to direct his ire with nauseating symbols of dirt, rot and stench in the first novel, *The Beautyful Ones Are Not Yet Born*. The 'Black Skin, White Masks' syndrome which infected every walk of life was appalling to the young intellectual which led to an inner conflict within the artist and his second novel, *Fragments* carries this burden.

Armah has been an infrequent visitor to Ghana. His visits to the other African countries have not been infrequent; he has lived in the east, west, north and southern Africa. The experience of post-colonial enuui and a deep sense of loss are well reflected in his third novel, *Why Are We So Blest*? Probably, it has much to do with his stint as a translator in Algeria, a homeground of African revolutionaries for a long time. Armah was a witness to the degeneration of values in the post-independent situation in Algeria. It was during his stay in Tanzania that he started writing *Two Thou-*

sand Seasons. The novel is a manifesto of a whole race and a counter-blast to colonialism of all hues.

The post-independent African situation is always plagued by political conflicts and coups d'etat. It is a sad saga of inner and intra-party struggles and corruption in high places. The political independence which became synonymous with neo-colonialism has left Africa at the mercy of imperialist forces and multi-national corporations. Thus, the far reaching ramifications of colonialism have created problems for Africa even after independence. What is particularly alarming about the whole situation is the fact that neither the nationalist leaders nor the subsequent military regimes provided an opportunity for the vast exploited masses to participate in the political processes. Besides, these regimes invariably worked for the legitimisation of the role of reactionary forces.

In the absence of a coherent ideology and clear-cut direction, fissiparious tendencies gained ground to subvert the revolutionary character of the masses. Imperialist forces, operating through economic programmes of their former colonies encouraged nascent divisive forces in the form of narrow parochialism, ethnic feuds and religious rivalries. The vast masses, instead of becoming instruments of change, became tools in the hands of their masters. The post-colonial situation has been best summed up by Zaya Yeebo with particular reference to the Ghanaian context:

> As the present state does not provide the right channels for workers and peasants to participate in the political process, trade unionism is the only avenue open to the workers. . . . In the rural areas, the ethnic movements and religious groups are strengthening their hold over the peasants. . . . The experience of Ghana . . . also points to the limits of populist nationalism which, rather than being a potential revolutionary force may be a specific mode of adoptation of a neo-colonial state in crisis to the logic of international capital.[1]

For Armah, this is only a temporary phase. The dynamics of social change would not permit the continuation of such a situation for a long time. He is of the view that bogus African nationalism would come to an end, once the transitional phase of the maimed leadership dies out. In his essay on 'African Socialism,' he prophesies the birth of two alternative forms of rule, one retrogressive and the other progressive. It would be either

> a backward, reactionary return to colonial patterns or a progressive revolution. . . . The first, the backward retrenchment, is so far the only logical step for which colonial and post-Independence experiences have been preparing the African people. The other alternative, a revolutionary restructuring of lines of authority, has only academic interest at this point. Classes exist in Africa. Furthermore, there are spectacular differences in standards of living and access to privileges and services provided through the use of common wealth of the states. So the dynamite is there. What is so far lacking is a widespread consciousness of connections between socio-economic inequalities and the structures of the social order. This consciousness cannot be learnt in hothouse institutions like so much Greek or Mathematics. It has to grow out of the visible, audible and sensible facts of life in each society, especially when these societies have hordes of poor people and yet enjoy politico-economic systems that encourage the growth of a propertied, prosperous minority. When this happens the naturally growing consciousness of people may be compared to a fuse. And it is only then that it makes sense for the revolutionary agitator to talk of striking a spark.[2]

Such an understanding of the dynamics of social transformation is also reflected by Armah in the fusion of different time frames and slices of history as discernible in his fiction. It is also marked by an awareness that the continent is alienated as a result of colonial brigandage and sabotage from within. Thus, the sense of alienation and exile in literary works is a natural corollary of the larger state of alienation of the society. Armah is greatly influenced by Martinican psychiatrist-revolutionary, Frantz Fanon, in respect of the latter's views on alienation and violence. With the intention of demonstrating to his fellow Africans the socio-psychological mechanisms which conceal the causes of their oppression, Fanon formulated his own experiences in the National Liberation Front in Algeria in a treatise entitled *The Wretched of the Earth.* Armah acknowledges the influence of Fanon in the following terms:

> The one theorist who has worked out consistent formulations concerning . . . a revolutionary restructuring of African society is Frantz Fanon.[3]

Although Fanon advocated an inter-disciplinary approach embracing psychological, sociological and economic methods of interpretation to expose colonial structures his stress was always on the psychological implications of the process of destabilization initiated by the colonizer and of the cluster of problems related to the levels of endurance and the process of restoration sustained by the colonized. Fanon's psychological-therapeutic approach is primarily concerned with the states of mind, the different kinds of frustrations and complexes which deny the natives an opportunity to view themselves as an entity, as a class and to gauge their economic plight.

The superiority of the colonizers has two dimensions: It manifests itself through brute force and coercion which is legitimized in their own view by the alleged inferiority of the natives. Secondly, it is acknowledged by the oppressed themselves through the process of alienation. Thus Fanon directs the attention of the black man towards the realization that his alienation is not an individual problem. Its causes can be found in the interiorization or epidermalization of an historically and economically determined inferiority.

Fanon emphasizes the significance of violence in the process of liberation of mind. The violence of the colonized is an act of emancipation. He finds his freedom in and through violence. It is his answer to the acts of coercion perpetrated against him. In the process of decolonization the colonized uses his act of violence as a restorative principle which is capable of freeing him from his reified status and making him once more a human being. Fanon's concept of violence as a cleansing force operates at two levels: it aims at dismantling the material structures of the colonial system and at another level breaks the psychological barrier and the alienation of the colonized.

Fanon identifies three social categories in the colonies: the peasantry which constitutes the mass of population, the proletariat in its embryonic form and the national bourgeoisie. He is of the view that the third group could be a menace to the very interests of the masses at any stage in the post-colonial era. In his analysis of this phenomenon, Fanon observes:

> The national bourgeoisie, since it is stung up to defend its immediate interests, and sees no farther than the end of its nose, reveals itself incapable of simply bringing national unity into being or of building up the nation on a stable and productive basis. The national front which has forced colonialism to withdraw cracks up and wastes the victory it has gained.[4]

The national bourgeoisie refuses to follow the path of revolution. After independence, it takes over and picks up the threads of colonialist tendencies and exploitative methods from their past masters. In the process, it also enlists the support of religious and racial prejudice.

The nationalist leader, instead of representing the aspirations of the people, tries to strangle the revolutionary spirit. His greed is not very dissimilar to that of the colonial masters. What Nuruddin Farah said in the eighties was prophesied by Fanon even before many African nations gained independence. According to Farah, "The African politician is a blind man: he moves in only one direction—towards himself."[5] Fanon prophesied that the inner purpose of the leader would be "to become the general president of that company of profiteers impatient for their returns."[6]

Colonialism, cultural imperialism and racial discrimination methodically denigrated the African society and culture. The theory that Africa was a dark continent and its inhabitants were primitives was propagated for a long time by the colonial masters. They systematically destroyed the indigenous systems and structures of the native institutions. Quite a few African writers, for instance, Achebe and Ngugi wa Thiong'o, have successfully dismantled the Western version of Africa through their fiction. They also demonstrated to the world that the pre-colonial African societies were harmonious, well-knit and that they had their own indigenous systems of governance aimed at egalitarianism. Chinua Achebe says that reclamation of the past and re-creation of history are fundamental to African literature:

> This theme put quite simply—is that African people did not hear of culture for the first time from Europeans; that their societies were not mindless but frequently had a philosophy of great depth and value and beauty, that they had poetry, and, above all, they had dignity. It is this dignity that many African people all but lost during the colonial period and it is this that they must now regain.[7]

It is clear from the above observation that an important facet of the traditional societies is its rich cultural heritage. Culture denotes the way of life of a people which determines their social and political systems as well as their material and spiritual values. In the process of evolution, culture helps to shape and modify the very thinking and intellect of its people. Dealing with this dialectical nature of culture, Jomo Kenyatta observes in his monumental work, *Facing Mount Kenya*:

> A culture has no meaning apart from the social organisation of life on which it is built. When the European comes to Gikuyu country and robs the people of their land, he is taking away not only their livelihood, but their material symbol that holds family and tribe together. In doing this, he gives one blow which cuts away the foundation from the whole Gikuyu life, social, moral, and economic.[8]

Culture by its very nature is not a static concept. It is always resilient and flexible. It manifests itself in the people's songs, dances and various art-forms at a given time. Above all, it fosters the spirit of the community and acts as a unifying principle.

The 'group concept' inherent in the oral traditions in a non-literate society is an example of this unifying principle. Africa has a rich oral tradition. It assumes a functional significance through rituals observed at birth, marriage and death. O.R. Dathorne brings out this element when he says:

> Most African literature, oral and written, may be so con-

> ceived as a cohesive whole because it is undertaken by groupspokesman for the group and on behalf of the group.[9]

When the modern African writer becomes a spokesman of his people, it is not very much different from that of an oral artist.

The cross-currents in the present African culture are traceable to Christian-European influence on the one hand and Arab-Islamic domination on the other. The influence of this aspect on the native people is often negative. The people were made the target of not merely political but social, economic and cultural hegemonism as well. Cultural exploitation was carried out through the imposition of alien religious and educational systems. Chiekh Hamidou Kane brings out this element of cultural imperialism when he observes: "Better than the cannon, it, the shool, makes conquest permanent. The cannon compels the body; the shool bewitches the soul."[10]

The colonial policy of the debasement of the colonized is designed in such a way as to make the natives look for protection in the changed context. The coloniser justifies his colonizing function as that of a progressive pioneer and promoter. The Christian Missionaries played an important role in this respect. The Missionaries condemned the religious customs and rituals of the natives as primitive and savage so as to impose their own religion. Fanon unmasks the real motto behind the religious propaganda. He observes:

> The Church in the colonies is the white people's church, the foreigner's church. She does not call the native to God's ways but to the ways of the white man, of the master, of the oppressor.[11]

Thus the early Christian Missionaries acted as the cultural middlemen between the coloniser and the natives.

II

It is one of the ironies that the African writer has to resort to the language of his colonizers even when the assault is directed against their values. The situation is reflected in the frantic search by the African writer for "some more specific corroboration of his vision through languages that can be consented to, or the authenticity of which can be attested to, by his people."[12] Ngugi wa Thiong'o is the foremost to champion this "search for a genuine homecoming."[13] In a bid "to break out of the linguistic prison to seek their genuine roots in the languages and rhythms of life of the dispossessed majority"[14] he himself has undertaken to writing in his own native language, Gikuyu.

The creation of the modern African state, a relatively new phenomenon, with its own tale of tears and blood during the colonial holocaust, provides ample scope for the creative novelists to constitute in writing the reconstruction of the past and documentation of the vicissitudes of African history. History—whether it is the distant past or the immediate present—has not been particularly kind to their people. This belief pervades the whole gamut of their writings and imagination. They feel an urge to portray the wounded feelings and hurt sentiments of a collective psyche. The African writers do not seem to believe in what E.W. Said calls "the protocol of pretended supra political objectivity."[15] Besides, they are good story tellers in the fashion of their oral artists in the pre-colonial and pre-literate societies.

In the pre-Independence years, African nationalists sought through their novels to recapture the spirit of the traditional institutions with their original dignity and coherence. Chinua Achebe's *Things Fall Apart* and *Arrow of God*, which are considered classics in this mould, present the historical perspective of a creative novelist performing the role of both a chronicler and a creator at the same time. Although he cannot be called an historian or an anthropologist in the strict sense of the term, he has successfully delineated the traditional Igbo life. In these two novels, one can find a nice mix of fiction and social vision. Such a 'restorative role' of the artist has been emphasized by Achebe himself in one of his interviews:

> What I am doing is presenting a total life as it is lived in that world and you cannot do that in a vacuum; I cannot do it in a vacuum. I am writing about my people in the past and in the present and I have to create for them the world in which they live and move and have their being. If somebody else

> thinks, as some do, that there is sociology, or anthropology that's their own lookout. It is the life of the people I am writing about. Therefore, if someone is in search of information, or knowledge, or enlightenment about the total life of these people—the Igbo people—I think my novels would be a good source.[16]

While dealing with the question of the 'successful homecoming' of African literature, Ngugi wa Thiong'o argues in one of his recent essays that it has already passed through at least three different phases in the last four decades. In the fifties, it echoed the sentiments of the people for independence. The sixties, the era of coups d'etat, gave birth to a literature of disillusionment. The seventies and the eighties saw more writers seeking to find a way out of earlier despair by 'trying to connect the works of the imagination with the struggles of the people for social change and social justice.'[17]

It is with such issues of 'social change' that Ngugi's *A Grain of Wheat*, Sembene Ousmane's *God's Bits of Wood* and Armah's *Two Thousand Seasons* are concerned. They also present a reconstruction of African history—either of fairly recent origin, often confined to a single event or of a remote past with a view to directing the focus on 'social justice.' *A Grain of Wheat* depicts the Kenyan nationalist struggle for independence. The novel presents an insider's account of the Mau Mau rebellion. Ngugi portrays in authentic terms the anti-colonial struggle as having been dominated by a nationalist sentiment and subverted by the agents of colonisers. Sembene Ousmane's novel, *God's Bits of Wood* which is a re-creation of the Niger-Dakar railway strike in 1947-48, has a Marxist dimension. The novel assumes epic proportions in that the heroic struggle is carried out collectively for the restoration of a sense of justice. The struggle itself becomes the hero of the novel in much the same way as the Mau Mau uprising plays a significant role in Ngugi's novel. In the same way, *Two Thousand Seasons* offers a picture of wholeness, while *The Healers* duly brings in inspiration. These novelists attempt to offer a way of life in positive terms through their fiction. The position of the writers as it emerges from these novels seems to attest the definition of art provided by Trotsky that "art is not a mirror, but a hammer: it does not reflect, it shapes."[18] These novelists attempt to indicate what features of the African traditional system are worth preservation. One can also discern the purpose of examining the past and reconstructing different historical phases through the medium of fiction in the words of Mumbi in *A Grain of Wheat*: 'together plan the future we want.'[19]

New experiments and innovations in technique, style and presentation were made by many African novelists in the seventies and eighties. These novelists no longer owe their allegiance to the classical tradition of the novel. For them, the form of the novel is no less important than its content. This search for a proper medium and style as discernible in the works of Soyinka, Oulouguem, Awoonor and Armah focusses light on the conflicts and tensions in society. At the same time, they draw inspiration from the traditional African art-forms. Despite their modernism, the African writers have not distanced themselves from the hard realities confronting the society. As Wole Soyinka rightly observes in *Myth, Literature and the African World*, the concerns have not changed very much but the novelist's choice of expression has gone a sea change:

> Much African writing is still rooted in the concept of literature as part of the normal social activity of man, but one which is nonetheless individual in its expression and its choice of areas of concern.[20]

It is this 'normal social activity of man' with 'its choice of areas of concern' and with its own 'ontology of idiom'[21] that substantiates the fictional world of Armah.

III

Ayi Kwei Armah speaks for and on behalf of his community. He dons the role of a teacher, curator and therapist for a whole community. While realising the function of a writer in the African context, Armah's fiction bears the stamp of the novelist with a vehemence of approach and a sense of urgency. This is what precisely distinguishes him from the other African novelists who are no less continental in their approach. His understanding of the African situation and the dynamics involved in the process of social change lend coherence and strength to his fictional medium. Armah's earlier novels present an irrepressible yearning for a complete breakaway from the present meaninglessness of neocolonialism. His later works stridently attempt to concretize the possibilities of hope and affirmation in fictional terms.

The complexity of African culture and history finds its profound expression in Armah's novels. The recurring complexity of the theme and the employment of native and western techniques render the total presentation of the panorama multi-coloured. The future of Africa is portrayed in the light of the present and the past. It is guided by an awareness on the part of Armah that the contemporary situation is rotten with its systematic demolition of the traditional institutions whereas the past paves the way for a long journey ahead. What Fanon observed in respect of the colonized writers is also applicable to Armah who is engaged in the task of decolonizing the mind:

> The colonized man who writes for his people ought to use the past with the intention of opening the future as an invitation to action and a basis for hope.[22]

Armah's work, in its totality, offers a study in aesthetic dialectics. If the novelist's visionary projection forms the thesis, the sordid reality presented in the first three novels provides aesthetics of negation. Synthesis is achieved in the wholesome and positive view as discernible in *Two Thousand Seasons* and *The Healers*. This process of dialectical progression is also evidenced in the development of each novel.

The first three novels of Armah, *The Beautyful Ones Are Not Yet Born*, *Fragments* and *Why Are We So Blest*? attempt a critical survey of the post-independent and neo-colonial context. The titles suggest the mood of the times. But this mood of disaffection and the sense of exile are a common and recurring phenomenon in many African writers. For instance, Achebe's *A Man of the People* and Soyinka's *The Interpreters*, in highly satirical terms, present the gloominess of the post-independent period. Armah's fourth novel, *Two Thousand Seasons* and his fifth novel, *The Healers* are an attempt at the recreation of history.

These two analytical and constructive stages in the literary creation of Armah are not mutually contradictory. This definite trend of evolution is effected by Armah by a shift of emphasis. For, the historical vision as discernible in the last two novels, is traceable to the first phase itself. The evolutionary process in Armah's novels is marked by a historical perspective. It is significant to note that the dialectical process of time frames and different phases of African history lend meaning and unity to each individual work. The real concerns of Armah emerge clearly only when these shifts are closely followed. The first three novels, for instance, deal with local realities, the alienation of individuals only to direct the attention to a more meaningful existence. Alienation, as such, is a part of alienation of the society resulting from the loss of a sense of community. In Armah, individualism has a place only in the context of community.

It follows quite naturally that the nationalist identity of a writer as exhibited in the first instance, need not be an impediment to his larger continental and Pan-African aspirations. In the visionary construct of Armah, the relationship between the specific and the general in the work of art on the one hand and between the local and continental realities in general gains in importance. In fact, Chidi Amuta observes that these two factors of unity become synonymous in the African context:

> The relationship between the national and continental imperatives in African literatures, re-echoes the theoretical relationship between the specific and the general in the identity of individual work of African literature. Each work of African literature created from a national perspective approaches the continental truth through a rigorous objectification of its specific national realities, for both realms of experience are dialectically and historically interconnected.[23]

Armah's work points to such a dialectical and historical interconnection between the two realms of experience which, in fact, helps to elevate the national perspective into 'continental truth.' This interaction also defines 'the way' of the group ethic as envisioned in his fictional creation—subtly suggested in the critical/analytical/national phase and explicitly enunciated in the historical/constructive/continental phase.

IV

It is useful to shed some light on the critical polarisation concerning Armah's brilliance as a novelist. The critical opinion mounted against Armah can be classified into two groups—colonialist and reductionist. Such criticism has its own pitfalls as it fails, sometimes refuses, to see reason beyond superficialities. Charles E. Nnolim introduces Armah as both a "cosmic pessimist" and "a retrogressive pejorist" for whom "Ghana is one giant, stinking lavatory."[24] According to him, Armah is "unusually excited by images of decay and corruption" and "thrives on the scenes of ooze, slime, rot and decay."[25] For him, Armah is a writer whose "philosophic pessimism is undisguised in each work." In this light, he analyses Armah's first three novels, choosing only those "linguistic clues" that dialectically structure each work and lend form to inevitably conclude that the centre is eventually a pejoristic and pessimistic one. Ben Obumselu comments that Armah expresees the "aesthetic discomfort of an American tourist" and "misanthropic neurosis" that was characteristic of "an exiled imagination."[26] According to Achebe, the first novel is "a sick book"[27] and the second "worse than the first and the third . . . worse than the second."[28] He describes Armah as an "alienated native . . . writing like some white District Officer."[29]

Reductionist criticism of this type stems from a refusal to accept the proposition that dialectial conception of art and society recognises the "aesthetics of negation."[30] Besides, Armah is performing the very roles of a teacher and a restorative artist as enunciated by Achebe himself. A skilful artist that he is, negation in the hands of Armah becomes more of a technique than a blur on the vision. It is a launching pad for the opening of new avenues and affirmation.

Colonialist criticism against Armah is prompted by racial prejudice and bias. This line of criticism is more pronounced against the last two novels. *Two Thousand Seasons*, in particular, attempts to dismantle the colonialist myths on Africa. Bernth Lindfors provides a case in point when he says that Armah's history or his version of it is "cartoon history" which "ultimately is not positive vision."[31] The structural and thematic polarities of good and evil depicted in his last two novels become for Lindfors a kind of

> . . . xenophobic oversimplification used to be found in B-grade films manufactured in Hollywood during the Second World War, in which fanatical kamikaze pilots and fat, stupid, goose-stepping German generals represented all that was reprehensible in the world. The 'Japs' and 'Krauts' in such celluloid fantasies performed essentially the same function as the 'predators' and 'destroyers' in Armah's fiction: they were crude, simplistic symbols towards which a chauvinistic audience could direct the energy of its hatred while waiting for the satisfying *denouement* in which vice would be vanquished and virtue rewarded. The good guy might lose a few battles but they always won the war.[32]

In *The Emergence of African Fiction*,[33] Charles Larson patronisingly reviews Armah's novels and compares his second novel, *Fragments* with *A Portrait of the Artist as a Young Man*. Armah who shuns interviews and essays on his own writings, in a rare departure takes Larson to task in 'Larsony or Fiction as Criticism of Fiction.' A fitting counterpoint has also been provided by Chidi Amuta to such colonialist criticism when he declares that they do not need value judgements from critics whose "political biases and aesthetic values are motivated from outside."[34] He considers Armah a 'brilliant' novelist.[35] Elsewhere, while examining Armah's treatment of the relationship between the African artist and society, he makes a pertinent point when he perceptively remarks that *Two Thousand Seasons* and *The Healers* "precede the others in a diachronic paradigm." He attempts to put Armah's historical novels in proper perspective, when he says:

> As novels of historical reconstruction both attempt to re-create the essence of pre-colonial African society in the light of contemporary experience.[36]

In addition to the two types of criticism against Armah, there is also yet another variety which tries to assess and evaluate Armah's fiction in a proper perspective. In the first-ever full-length study of Armah's novels,[37] Robert Fraser argues that Armah's novels are misread because these critics are desperate to protect themselves against the unpalatability of the disclosed truths. Consequently, they approached 'defensively' to Armah's art to blunt the thrust of its vision. He seems to be of the view that Armah's critics are guilty of grafting their own culturally derived 'individualistic humanist' aesthetic onto Armah's 'communalistic' art. Fraser attempts to posit the drive of Armah's vision in a positive frame but his own interpretation of the individual novels is flawed in some respects. The positive thrust of Armah's earlier novels eludes him as he undermines the unyielding struggle of the man in *The Beautyful Ones Are Not Yet Born*. It is also evidenced in his insensitivity to the promise of regeneration sustained through the consciousness of Juana in *Fragments*. The bearer of affirmation and liberation is relegated to the status of an incidental character by Fraser. The fact, however, remains that Fraser has presented a picture which helps to appreciate Armah as a gifted writer with penetrating and wide ranging vision.

A failure by most of Armah's critics to perceive the basic theoretical dynamics of his vision, which is at once moral and humanistic, has led to much of misreading of his works. Soyinka's observations, in this context, help to enlighten the understanding of Armah's novels. While examining the writers' response to cultural situation, he makes a classification of African novelists.[38] In the frame of social vision he comes to represent, Armah is categorised as belonging to an exclusive category of "the uncompromising iconoclastic view."[39] Armah is shown sharply differing from Oulouguem's 'Iconoclasm' represented in his act of demolishing "all claims by all cultures and religions to any value pre-eminence or indeed, historic probity." Oulouguem reduces all cultures and civilisations—Arab-Islamic, European-Imperialist, black-dynastic and medieval and Christian—to the level of the absurd and they are 'paraded in a violent course of collision.' In sharp contrast, Armah's thoughts are based on strong ideological foundations. Soyinka holds that Armah's careful construction of a mythical past is "a potential model for the future."

The secular vision in African writing is aggressive and it finds its finest exponent in Armah. In his writings, the vision is guided by a moral and humanistic ethic. The secular vision in Armah and its ramifications have been stressed by Soyinka:

> The secular vision in African creative writing is particularly aggressive wherever it combines the re-creation of a pre-colonial African world view with eliciting its transposable elements into a modern potential. The process may be explicit, as in Armah's *Two Thousand Seasons*, or . . . may rely in the reader's capacity for projection. The shared knowledge of what now exists and the prior assumption of a readership subjectively attuned to the significations of posed comparisons is part of the armoury of the novel, which depending on the moralities of the conflicts and events does away with the need for utopian presentations. Assuming an unsympathetic readership, it remains a threat, a potent one, because its justifying paradigm has been woven from the authentic heritage of the society. The greater the realism, the more dangerous it appears to be.[40]

Soyinka's observation also provides a fitting reply to the colonialist-reductionist criticism launched against Armah. The 'armoury' of a novel includes the visionary projection of the author as well as the reader's capacity for projection. This helps to understand why Armah's novels met with an 'unsympathetic readership' and how these were lacking in 'the shared knowledge' and 'the prior assumption of a readership subjectively attuned.'

V

Armah's vision is not guided by a rigid set of beliefs and theoretical propositions nor is it conditioned by a blind adherence to Marxist beliefs separated from local realities. As his fictional works bear testimony, his moral vision is integral to his humanistic outlook. As the ensuing discussion reveals, Armah's works embody his profound concern for his people, his race and his continent. His moral outlook is underlined by a pragmatic socialist ideal.

Armah's moral vision is reflected in the pursuit of the journey as adhered to by a hero in each of the novels. He tries to lead, if passively on some occasions, either by personal example or direct action to the life-exuding path. But the disease is so deep-rooted that the hero is almost destroyed on some occasions by the very society that he wishes to serve. Modin in *Why Are We So Blest?* and Isanusi in *Two Thousand Seasons* actually die in the attempt. Baako in *Fragments* is driven to madness for following a path accepted as part of the system not so long ago but which is considered a taboo by the self-seeking contemporaries.

In spite of the seemingly passive posture adopted by the heroes in the first three novels, and the impending havoc wrought out by the society, all hope is not lost. The torch is carried on by those who have an imaginative rapport with the protagonists. In *Fragments,* Naana and Juana are constructing what Araba and Efua are destroying. In *The Healers,* Ajoba partakes in the process of healing. This introduces yet another dominant motif in the novels of Armah. The principle of feminine fertility emphasizes the regenerative force which provides inspiration and comfort to the hero.

The underlying motif of onward journey pervades all of Armah's novels but the techniques he employed are varied and divergent: direct statement, juxtaposition, biting satire, overstatement, photographic framing and a variety of symbols and motifs operating at various levels. The dynamics of structure and technique strengthen the content of the novel, while the content and form derive strength from and enrich the understanding of the context.

Armah's first novel, *The Beautyful Ones Are Not Yet Born*, with its predominantly urban setting in which the anonymous hero passively protests against the deterioration in value-systems in the society, belongs to the analytical stage. Armah has invested the surroundings of Ghana with all the conceivable images of decay, rot and corruption. These images leave behind a nauseating experience, making the desire for change all the more intense. It also helps to create an urgency for the affirmation of the cherished ideals. The shock treatment is a technique employed chiefly for the purpose of celebrating, what should have been, the real aspirations of the community. The man cannot see reason and meaning in the present social order but he is prepared to look forward to a future which lends beauty to the individual existence.

The search for a technique which effectively reflects the conflicts, inner and outer, is continued in *Fragments* and *Why Are We So Blest*? The cinematic techniques of freeze shots, close-up, flashback are exploited to the fullest extent in these novels. *Fragments* deals with the collapse of dreams of Baako, a sensitive artist, in a ramshackle society of fragmented vision. In a way, he is an heir to the man of the first novel. But Baako's struggle becomes more violent and vocal. While focussing the attention on a degenerate society, the novel attempts to strike a balance between individualism and social order. The shift to communal experience is evidenced in the soothing influence and old world wisdom of Naana and also the principle of feminine fertility embodied in Juana.

Armah's third novel, *Why Are We So Blest*?, examines the racial implications projected through personal relationships. The cumulative impact of psychological, political and sociological factors makes the blacks all along subservient to the whites who put their exploitative skills to their best advantage when it comes to the crunch. The novel is an indictment of the group ethic which fatally draws itself to the inhuman manipulation of the whites as evidenced in the relationship of Modin and Aimee. The political fate of such a group ethic is presented in terms of husband-mistress relationship.

Two Thousand Seasons, in an epic sweep, attempts to designate 'the way' of the people of a continent in the process of reclamation of the past one thousand years. The emphasis throughout the novel has been on the need to replace the dependence on the alien culture which proved disastrous for the natives. The assault in this novel is directed against the Arab-Islamic predators and Christian-European-Imperialist destroyers and also against the betrayers among the native people. The shift of emphasis takes the form of direct statement. The longing for creation becomes more explicit in the exuberant optimism conveyed through the symbols of river, stream and vegetation.

The Healers, together with *Two Thousand Seasons* could be viewed as offering positive response to the morbid scenario of reality as portrayed in the first three novels. *The Healers*, in particular, attempts to project the visionary ideal of Armah as understood by the still to be born beautiful ones of the first novel. It deals with the disintegration of the Asante empire during the late nineteenth century and provides a healing touch to a battered psyche ravaged by colonialism. It also introduces a new novelistic technique in the form of oral narration which turns out to be a path-breaker in the art of fiction.

In the light of these arguments, a critical analysis of the works of Armah is undertaken in the following chapters with particular reference to the integration achieved between the two interlinked phases of analytical and constructive novels, between content and form and also between authorial ideology and structural rhythms. The study attempts to prove Armah as a committed writer who has given a new thrust to the fusion of artistic excellence and ideological vision through the medium of fiction.

NOTES

1. Zaya Yeebo, "Ghana: Defence Committees and The Class Struggle," *Review of African Political Economy* (issue devoted to 'Intellectual and the Left in Africa'), No. 32 (April 1985), p. 72.
2. Ayi Kwei Armah, "African Socialism: Utopian or Scientific?," *Presence Africaine*, No. 64 (1967), p. 29.
3. *Ibid.*
4. Frantz Fanon, *The Wretched of the Earth* (London: Penguin Books, 1967), p. 128.
5. Nuruddin Farah, "The Creative Writer and the African Politician," *The Guardian* (9 September 1983), p. 11.
6. Frantz Fanon, p. 133.
7. Chinua Achebe, "The Role of the Writer in a New Nation," *African Writers on African Writing*, ed. G.D. Killam (London: Heinemann, 1972), p. 8.
8. Jomo Kenyatta, *Facing Mount Kenya* (London: Secker and Warburg, 1938), p. 317.
9. O.R. Dathorne, *African Literature in the Twentieth Century* (Minneapolis: University of Minnesota Press, 1974), p. x.
10. As quoted by Ngugi wa Thiong'o, *Homecoming* (London:

Heinemann, 1972), p. 10.
11. Frantz Fanon, p. 34.
12. Lewis Nkosi, *Tasks and Masks* (Essex: Longman Group, 1981), p. 6.
13. Ngugi wa Thiong'o, "From the Corridors of Silence," *The Weekend Guardian* (21-22 October 1989), p. 4.
14. *Ibid*.
15. Edward W. Said, *Orientalism* (London: R.K.P., 1978), p. 10.
16. Chinua Achebe, "An Interview with Chinua Achebe" by Kalu Ogbaa, *Research in African Literatures*, Vol. 10 (Spring, 1981), p. 1.
17. Ngugi wa Thiongo, "From the Corridors of Silence," p. 4.
18. As quoted by J.I. Okonkwo, "Cultural Revolution and the African Novel," *UFAHAMU*, Vol. XIV, No. 3 (1985), p. 108.
19. Ngugi wa Thiong'o, *A Grain of Wheat* (London: Heinemann, African writers series, 1967), p. 247.
20. Wole Soyinka, *Myth, Literature and the African World* (London: Cambridge University Press, 1976), p. 67.
21. *Ibid*., p. 64.
22. Frantz Fanon, p. 187.
23. Chidi Amuta, *The Theory of African Literature* (London: Zed Books, 1989), p. 67.
24. Charles E. Nnolim, "Dialectic as Form: Pejorism in the Novels of Armah," *African Literature Today*, No. 10 (1987), p. 207.
25. *Ibid*., p. 208.
26. Ben Obumselu, "Marx, Politics and the African Novel," *Twentieth Century Studies*, No. 10 (1973), p. 115.
27. Chinua Achebe, "Africa and Her Writers," *Morning Yet on Creation Day* (London: Heinemann, 1975), p. 25.
28. Chinua Achebe, "Class Discussion," *In Person: Achebe, Awoonor and Soyinka at the University of Washington*, ed. Karen Morell (Seattle, Institute of Comparative Studies, University of Washington, 1975), p. 52.
29. Chinua Achebe, "Africa and Her Writers," p. 52.
30. Chidi Amuta, *The Theory of African Literature*, p. 28.
31. Bernth Lindfors, "Armah's Histories," *African Literature Today*, No. 11 (1985), p. 90.
32. *Ibid*.
33. Charles Larson, "The Novel of the Future: Wole Soyinka and Ayi Kwei Armah," *The Emergence of African Fiction* (Hong Kong: Macmillan, 1971), pp. 242-77.
34. Chidi Amuta, *The Theory of African Literature*, p. 20.
35. *Ibid*., p. 59.

36. Chidi Amuta, "Portraits of the Contemporary Artist in Armah's Novels," *World Literature Written in English*, Vol. 21, No. 3 (Autumn 1982), p. 468.
37. Robert Fraser, *The Novels of Ayi Kwei Armah* (London: Heinemann, 1980).
38. Wole Soyinka, "Cross-Currents: The 'New African' After Cultural Encounters," *Writers in East-West Encounters: New Cultural Bearings* (London: Macmillan, 1982), pp. 51-63.
39. *Ibid.*, p. 54.
40. Wole Soyinka, *Myth, Literature and the African World*, p. 115.

The Waking of the Powerless: *The Beautyful Ones Are Not Yet Born*

Ayi Kwei Armah's first novel, *The Beautyful Ones Are Not Yet Born*[1] marked the advent of a major talent on the African literary scene. For those who held that African novel must develop its uniqueness by reflecting its traditional forms and concerns, the novel came as a shock. Partly for that reason and partly because of the controversial issues involved in the novel, it received considerable critical attention. Armah's concern for the survival of social norms and moral values coupled with his extensive use of symbol and image and his poetic use of language became the subject of discussion for a long time.

It is significant to note that the earlier critics and reviewers were very hostile to the novel and condemned it as an expression of despair and disillusionment. For them, the picture that the novel presents is that of a dark haven, an unbearably pessimistic, an unabashedly pejoristic, or worse, in the context of Ghana, an uncalled for existentialist world. It is only fairly recently that the novel came to be viewed in a favourable light and the 'beauty' of the novel came to be appreciated.

A closer look at the novel reveals the care and concern with which Armah has expressed his sense of commitment to his people. The novel has a carefully woven symbolic structure. The dialectical relationship between the novel and its context, its form and content, and the interplay between the past and present shape the course of the novel. Foremost among the critics of the novel is Chinua Achebe who concedes that this is a powerfully written novel with an admirable command of language and imagery. However, Achebe calls it a "sick book" in which, "the hero, pale and passive and nameless—a creation in the best manner of existentialist writing, wanders through the story in an anguished sleep, neck-deep in despair and human excrement of which we see rather a lot in the book."[2]

Eldred Jones in his review of the novel considers the dominant mood of the novel as one of "hopeless despair" with the author's "almost Swiftian preoccupation with the bodily secretions."[3] He concludes by saying: "Armah has taken the predicament of Africa in general, Ghana in particular, and distilled its despair and its hopelessness in a very powerful, harsh, deliberately unbeautyful novel."[4] While commenting on the novel, Charles Nnolim says:

> Symbolically, Armah's Ghana is Dante's Inferno, and much of the events take place in the circles of the avaricious, the gluttonous and the lustful, which contains sinners who are aptly appeased with dirt and filth and who stink in the mire of their own corruption.[5]

The extent of misunderstanding of Armah's first novel can be seen from the following two comments: one, which holds Armah guilty for the lack of what in fact is his major concern. The other finds fault with him for portraying what really exists. Emmanuel Obeichina, in his review of the novel, says:

> On the level of parable, it might pass but on the particularized level of fact, it raises numerous weighty questions which, given the limitations of the fictional medium, cannot be adequately dealt with. Maybe Armah has not heard of the word 'neocolonialism' or how it operates on the African man and on the African political destiny. Maybe he underrates what has been called 'the colonialism of the mind.[6]

When Armah's major themes—'neo-colonialism' and 'colonialism of the mind' are diligently portrayed in his fictional medium, the attitude to approach the novel in terms of parable and allegory blunts the very purpose of the novel. Shatto Arthur Gakwandi, while saying that "the senses of the reader are vigorously assaulted to the point of being numbed by the persistent imagery of decay, putrefaction and death," complains that "the novel dismisses the black elite as slaves of the colonial boss and their only ambition to take over the privileges of their former masters."[7] Lewis Nkosi, while holding a diametrically opposite point of view, says that such an observation is borne out of "obtuse prejudice" and defends Armah: "I dare say many will find nothing essentially wrong with such a picture of the modern elite in Africa."[8]

Nkosi considers the remarks of Achebe "rather reprovingly school-masterish." The novel, according to Nkosi, is written "in the best protest tradition, with a message that is wider and more profound in its significance than is usually the case in many novels of this kind."[9] O.R. Dathorne characterizes the novel as a "milestone," which is "individualised in style and language, radical in thought and frightening in its frank and fearless realism."[10] Robert Fraser points out the historical dimension of the book, observable from two angles: "The short perspective of recent Ghanaian politics and the longer perspective of a centuries-old cultural betrayal."[11] Neil Lazarus, in his aptly titled essay, "Pessimism of the Intellect and Optimism of the Will," says that the novel is "couched as a voyage of discovery," which ultimately turns out to be "preeminently a dialectical work."[12] For Rand Bishop, the novel "remains one of the most tightly constructed and powerful novels of any literature and century."[13]

It is in this context of polarization of critical opinion that a careful analysis of the novel gains in importance. The dialectical relationship between the vision of Armah and the actual "blasted landscape," in a structural pattern that is at once baffling and flamboyant requires a closer scrutiny. Coming back to Achebe's criticism of the novel, the answer for it is not far to seek. In one of his interviews, Achebe says:

> we all admit that there is a lot to protest against in every community, in every civilization. If things were perfect, there would be no need for writers to write their novels. But it is because they see a vision of the world which is better than what exists, it is because they see the possibilities of man rising higher than he has risen at the moment that they write. So, whatever they write, if they are true practitioners of their art, would be in essence a protest against what exists, what is.[14]

Armah's vision of the world is certainly better than 'what exists' and he sees infinite possibilities of man 'rising higher' than at the present moment. What prompts him to portray decay and degeneration with all its allusory motifs is a deep-rooted feeling of pain and hurt. As a result, we are compelled to see that the African history is a continuous story of exploitation and betrayal first by one master, and then by another. The pungent satire in this novel is directed particularly against the latter category whom Fanon describes in a title of his treatise as "Black Skin, White Masks" and whom Armah himself terms as "Black Masters, White Shadows." Fanon's theory of neo-colonialism has far-reaching implications and his perceptive comments help us put the novel in its proper perspective. He says:

> The national bourgeoisie of underdeveloped countries is not engaged in production, nor in invention, nor building, nor labour; it is completely canalized into activities of the intermediary type. Its innermost vocation seems to be to keep in the running and to be part of the racket. The psychology of the national bourgeoisie is that of the businessman, not that of a captain of industry.[15]

The decay and rot are so blatant in contemporary Ghana, and its corruption so rampant, that one is constantly drawn to Fanon's portents even before many African nations gained independence. Armah realizes that the prophecy came to be true with devastating effect and his first novel is a manifestation of this realization of the 'obscene haste' (88) with which it materialized. It is with the businessman-like psychology of the national bourgeoisie and their "activities of the intermediary type" that Armah deals in this novel with the clinical precision of a surgeon. Armah also decries the nationalist leaders for their greed and acquisitiveness. He says:

> African politicians love flashy scenes and high-flauntin' words. That is only a partial exploration. More important is the historical fact that in a very radical sense the nationalist leaders of Africa have found themselves sucked into the role of hypocrites, actions involved in a make-believe situation.[16]

Armah's preoccupation with the dislocation of ideals in the aftermath of independence adds to the novel a political, and in the larger perspective a historical dimension to the dialectical processes at work. The Nkrumah regime in Ghana which started off on a note of promise, slided into a mire of corruption and degeneration. The political leadership and the bureaucracy vied with each other in pursuit of selfish gains and comforts at the expense of the gullible people. The people also showed a tendency to imitate their former colonial masters and nationalist leaders.

The unnamed protagonist of the novel is an ordinary railway clerk at Takoradi, leading a dull and drab life. However, he is set apart from others by his two redeeming qualities. In the first place, he is sharp and perceptive and is invested with "a mind and body which together form the nerve-centre of a radio-active kind of searchlight."[17] He is often amazed by the 'squat massiveness' of his office-building. He could also observe the 'great deal of care' that went into the 'making of even the bricks' (11). This sensitive perception enables him to closely observe men and manners, helps him in his judgement of the beautiful and the ugly and the moral choice between good and bad.

Secondly, the man is alive to the social realities, particularly the problem of corruption which is not only rampant but seems ineradicable in the given context. He prefers to keep himself aloof from the mad crowds who are on the look-out for personal gains and comforts at any cost. He is unwilling to take part in the 'national game' (129) of corruption and self-promotion.

It is important to note that the man is the inheritor of the traditional ideals and values. But it is the man who is forced to be a stranger in spite of himself. His family nags him for his lack of punch and the society dismisses him with contemptuous indifference. In one of his confessional moments, the man informs Teacher: 'I am the one who feels strange' (54). His 'movement'—both physical and moral—is natural, but is always faced with the peculiar situation of being labelled 'unnatural' by the society. It views his attempts at preserving his own integrity with a perverse logic, since it considers 'there was too much of the unnatural in any man who imagines he could escape the inevitable decay of life and accept the decline into final disintegration' (47-48).

The predicament of the man is strikingly contrasted with the rapid fortunes his childhood friend, Koomson, has made in the hierarchy of social and political echelons. He reads the pulse of the people and exploits the prevailing situation to his fullest advantage. His success story from that of a dock-worker to the position of a minister through manipulative skills testifies to his belief in easy gain. Koomson is a total violation of everything his party stands for. His money-making schemes prompt him to declare that socialism is a 'nuisance' (136). The hypocrisy of the regime is brought out when he confesses that 'the old man (Nkrumah) himself does not believe in it' (136). With all his moral depravity, Koomson comes to symbolize the ethos of a whole nation in the given context.

The man, on the other hand, scrupulously follows the norms and principles of the party. He is not alone in his pursuit of a life that opens up possibilities for all. He frequently visits one of his friends, Teacher, from whom he seeks advice and guidance. Teacher remains literally naked and aloof. The social oblivion Teacher has imposed upon himself has much to do with disaffection with the post-independent situation. The degradation in all walks of life as a result of the 'easy slide' (31) towards the 'blinding gleam' (56) forces him to adopt a lonely posture. He realizes that he cannot redeem it, and so redeems himself in his own way by not participating even in the normal social activity. He withdraws into his shell of isolation in which his freedom is indistinguishable from its non-existence. He says:

> It [freedom] makes no difference. If we can't consume ourselves for something we believe in, freedom makes no difference at all. You see, I am free to do what I want, but there is nothing happening now that I want to join. (61)

By making a statement on his own freedom, Teacher provides a fitting commentary on Ghana's independence as well.

While conversing with the man, Teacher remembers in a flashback his two old friends who shared his revolutionary fervour—Maanan, the prostitute, and Kofi Billy, the dock-worker who had lost his leg doing work 'that was too cruel to white men's hands' (65). They smoked 'wee' together and 'swallowed all the keen knowledge of betrayal' (65). It was Maanan who enthusiastically greeted the 'new one' (Nkrumah) and saw a new ray of hope in him. But soon their expectations are belied and Teacher is forced to comment: 'How could this have grown rotten with such obscene haste?' (88). Kofi Billy commits suicide, Maanan turns mad and Teacher withdraws into his shell with the realization that

> There is no difference then. No difference at all between the white men and their apes, the lawyers and the merchants, and now the apes of the apes, our Party men. (89)

Maanan, even in her madness, is concerned with the plight of the people. She is last heard as saying: "They have mixed it all together! Everything! They have mixed everything." (180)

Thus Teacher, Maanan and Kofi Billy have an imaginative rapport with the man. But forced by circumstances, they withdraw into their respective shells—Teacher in his literal and symbolic frozenness, Maanan in madness and Kofi Billy in death. The onus lies entirely on the man to show a positive frame of mind to carry on his lonely struggle. A witness to the two extreme worlds—the frozen seclusion of Teacher and the ambitious 'drive' of Koomson—the man's balancing factor gains importance. It is shown in his natural 'walking.' He does not like to model himself upon the posture of stillness adopted by Teacher. While analysing the situation, the man strikes at the root of the inner conflict which at times undermines his role as an active participant in the struggle against 'the gleam.' He says: 'I have my family. I am in the middle.' (93)

By the same token, the man cannot be a party to the driving ambitions exhibited by Koomson and his wife, Estella. They have 'grown fat with spoils of office.' The man's position is vindicated and his paradox resolved by the ultimate downfall of Koomson, and his regime in a coup that forces him to take the help of the man. Thus the false facade of the gleam is exposed. But there is little hope even in the new dispensation. And so, the question still remains whether the beautiful ones will ever be born. The man prepares to resume his routine, hopefully waiting for the arrival of the beautiful ones. Despite all the pressures and adverse conditions, the man has his integrity intact and comes out of the ordeal unscathed.

II

It is a sad commentary of the prevailing state of things that the man who cherishes the norms and values in public life and who recognizes the role of a responsible citizen in a socialist country should be a loner, whereas the person who blatantly violates the norms of social welfare and hankers after personal comforts should be adored for his meteoric rise in the hierarchy and the skills he employed to get into that position. Teacher wonders: "Here we have had a kind of movement that should make even good stomachs go sick. What is painful to the thinking mind is not the movement itself, but the dizzying speed of it" (62).

For the thinking mind, this is a kind of 'irresistible horror' in which everybody seemed to sweat a lot, 'not from the exertion of their jobs, but from some kind of inner struggle that was always going on' (20). There is a scramble for 'the upward climb' (20). In other words, it is a kind of 'living death' from which there seems to be no escape. Even the efforts one made not to join the mad race resulted in another kind of frustration.

The man's predicament is portrayed in internal and external terms. The internal situation is characterized by his stubborn refusal to accept and adopt the vicious game of corruption. It is also characterized by an awareness that there are not many people like him. Consequently, he admonishes himself for being an odd man out in the total pattern of social behaviour and moral ethos of a particular phase. Two factors emerge out of this observation, one causative and the other resultant. First, the self-admonishing attitude of the man:

> The man was left alone with thoughts of the easy slide, and how everything said there was something miserable, something unspeakably dishonest about a man who refused to take and to give what everyone around was busy taking and giving; something unnatural, something very cruel, something that was criminal for who but a criminal could ever be left with such a feeling of loneliness? (31-32)

The corrupting influence of the gleam has imposed itself upon the world as reality and the man finds himself in the company of the living dead. Such feelings of unease in the man can be attributed to the eroding influence of the 'gleam' over the vision of moral intelligence. The partial success of this operation can be seen from the isolation of the man and his occasional attraction for the same, if only for the sake of his family. While examining his own inner conflicts and his own pressing need to possess the gleam, primarily forced by the needs of his family, the man says:

> The gleam, in moments of honesty, had a power to produce a disturbing ambiguity within. It would be good to say that the gleam never did attract. It would be good, but it would be far from truth. And something terrible was happening as time went on. It was getting harder to tell whether the gleam repelled more than it attracted, attracted more than it repelled, or just did both at once, in one disgustingly confused feeling all the time these heavy days. (10)

The gleam, accepted by the mainstream of a whole nation, is capable of creating conflicting tendencies even in those who wish to follow a path of honesty. The reason for this self-admonishment in the man and the resultant passive resistance can be attributed to his culture, upbringing and more precisely, his affection for his family—'the land of the loved ones.' This affection for the family both accentuates his feeling of desperation and loneliness and also undermines his role as an active participant in his lonely struggle. His love for his children is exemplified in his act of refusal to take more meat so that they will have more to eat.

The resultant aspect of this very human trait is that it saves the protagonist from being cast into a type and the novel as well from becoming a parable. When his wife says that the life Estella leads is a nice and clear one, the man replies in a manner that underlines decisiveness of his attitude: "Some of that kind of clearness has more rottenness in it than the slime at the bottom of a garbage dump" (44). Thus, the self-conflicting attitude in the man is borne out of a fit of compulsion rather than a genuine wish to possess 'the gleam.'

The three movements of personal, social and political factors run parallel in the novel and they converge on a complex pattern. The personal dimension is sought to be mirrored by way of

Teacher's nakedness which itself marks his transition from a state of dynamism to a mere total impasse. Koomson is the epitome of the social movement as his is a story of success all the way by means of corruption and violation of the party ideology. The political factor and its ramifications are symbolised in Maanan's madness, which itself is a result of her absolute disillusionment with Nkrumah. Along with others, she thought of him as the Osagyefo, the redeemer. Above all, there is the moral factor, the man's incorruptible social vision that offers a stark contrast and a fitting counterpoint to the ongoing process of self-betrayal. The man is a keen watcher, a sharp commentator and an impartial judge of men and manners.

The man's participation in the struggle against the gleam should be viewed in the background of the spiritual vacuum. The fragmentation and unconnectedness seem to have affected even the things the people handle: 'When he struck a pencil into the sharpener and turned the handle, the handle sped round and round with the futile freedom of a thing connected to nothing else' (17). This search for connectedness and a valid identity elevates the stature of the protagonist. This strikingly individual thinking is reflected in his refusal, in the opening pages of the novel, to take the bribe offered by a timber contractor to make arrangments in the railway wagon for space allocation. Later, he becomes a witness to the scene of bribing the allocation clerk and others in the office.

This theme of corruption is also evident in the bankrupt policies of the government such as running a lottery. The system of lottery is a sad commentary at two levels: on the one hand, it reduces the poorest of the poor to squander a substantial part of their marginal income on buying lottery tickets. On the other hand, it also expresses the hollowness and corrupt policies of the state, a socialist state in the given context. This phenomenon is effectively demonstrated by the messenger working for the Ghanaian railways. Although he wins his lottery ticket, he is not sure of getting the prize amount as he is not in a position to bribe the officials concerned. Nor is it possible for him to enlist the support of the police for his cause. The sad truth of all this is very well summed up by his own comments when he says: "It costs you more money if you go to the police."

The historical vision of the novel is duly attested by its imagery. The robustness of language and delicacy of image attribute a sense of immediacy to its objects. The interplay of content and form and the dialectical interaction between the context and the work suggest the possibilities of a creative genius at work. The oft-quoted wood passage bears an ample testimony to his poetic rendering of a prose which finds its fullest expression in *Two Thousand Seasons*. The passage reads:

> The wood underneath would win and win till the end of time. Of that there was no doubt possible, only the pain of hope perennially doomed to disappointment. It was so clear. Of course, it was in the nature of the wood to rot with age. The polish, it was supposed, would catch the rot. But of course in the end it was the rot which imprisoned everything in its effortless embrace. It did not really have to fight. Being was enough. In the natural course of things it would always take the newness of the different kinds of polish and the vaunted cleansing power of the chemicals in them, and it would convert all to victorious filth, awaiting yet more polish again and again and again. And the wood was not alone. (12)

The description of the banister implies that the man is waging a futile struggle since it was in the nature of the wood to 'rot with age.' Previous experiences have shown that such exercises—hopeful struggles—are doomed 'to disappointment.' Immediately preceding the above passage, it was mentioned that 'What had been going on there and was going on now and would go on and on through all the years ahead was a species of war carried on in the silence of long ages.' (12). However, another reading of the passages which occur in the last pages of the first chapter reveals that the incantatory repetition of the words and dialectical interplay between wood, rot and polish paves the way for the final assertion—a repetition of the first sentence, but without the conditional situation reflected in the words, 'pain of hope' and 'doomed to disappointment'—and possibilities of hope: 'The wood would always win.' Within the context of rot and decay, all hope is not lost.

The details such as mentioned above are important in the novel because they offer vigour to the novel and render wholeness to the context. Kolawole Ogungbesan writes thus: "The deliberate sensuosity of [Armah's] style has no aesthetic value in itself; its values lie in the subtle means by which sensuous details become symbols, and in the way the symbols provide a network which is the story, and which simultaneously provides the writer and reader with a refined moral insight by means of which to evaluate it."[18]

The symbolism in the novel is both evocative and descriptive. Many critics pointed out that the dominant motif in the novel is decay and rot, what with the frequent mentioning of ooze, dirt, excreta which obviously represent the mess and disillusionment of the modern Ghanaian society. They inevitably concluded that the extensive use of such symbols portray nothing but despair, anguish and alienation of an individual. Such symbols are extensively made use of to intensify the nauseating atmosphere and suffocating attitudes. The novel is much more than this. A few critics have tried to point out the positive features which are integral to the novel. For instance, Kolawole Ogungbesan observes that the dominant motif of the novel is that of "life as a journey, specified here as road journey."[19]

Neil Lazarus who interprets the novel in terms of the primary motif of the novel, 'the gleam,' says that there are only two ways of living against the gleam: "The first of these is to concede the central province of reality to it" and the second is to "refuse to accept its domination of social reality, to campaign against it."[20] In the novel, Teacher, Maanan and Rama Krishna follow the first course by retreating into their marginality and the latter strategy is adopted by the man.

There is yet another dominant motif in the novel, which has eluded the critics so far, and which in fact, forms the life line of not merely *The Beautyful Ones Are Not Yet Born* but Armah's work as a whole. Water, which is at once a symbol of life-sustenance is also the source of inspiration. Armah's protagonists are constantly drawn to water and its attendant motifs of sea, river, and sand. In this novel, it is pitted against the 'blinding gleam' (56). The novel deals extensively with the gleam as Neil Lazarus points out, but the positive affirmation as exemplified in water lends coherence to the novel.

> Even from the small height of the dam, the water hit the bottom of the ditch with sufficient force to eat away the soft soil down to the harder stiff beneath, exposing a bottom of smooth sandy pebbles with the clear water now flowing over it. He drew back his gaze and was satisfied with the clearness of a quick attraction, not at all like the ambiguous disturbing tumult within awakened by the gleam. Somehow, there seemed to be a purity and a peace here which the gleam could never bring. (23)

The flow of water in a natural, unending and beautiful manner is strikingly contrasted with the artificial, twisted and glinting gleam. It is this natural flow that provides moments of comfort and solace for Teacher also:

> The water and the sand were active for me then; the water coming in long slow movements stretching back into ages so very long years ago and the land always answering the movement, though in our dead moments we do not have eyes to see any of this. (72)

But unfortunately neither is there such reciprocity nor harmony between the ideas of the individuals and imperative needs of the society. Sometimes, the fullness of the natural process reduces everything and everyone to nothing:

> The sand looked so beautiful then, so many little individual grains in the light of the night, giving the watcher the childhood feeling of infinite things finally understood, the humiliating feeling of watcher's nothingness. (72)

Teacher, in his interaction with Maanan, realizes the driving force of the feminine principle and its beauty, but he regrets that mankind has not been able to use its advantages well. The cleansing nature of sand and salt water is complimentary to the fertility motif of the feminine factor. These are portrayed in unifying terms:

> I could not help it as the moist sand dripped through my weakened fingers and joined the shore. Like an animal I knelt down and stretched out my hand to wash the sand away with the farthest coming of water of the waves, and then suddenly I felt like taking the salt water into my mouth. It was not only salt I tasted, but a hundred other strong things in the water and I cleansed my mouth with it and spat it out slowly and did it all again. Something that did not want to die made me touch Maanan softly on the side of her mouth. (73)

The images of preservation and fertility are followed by those of dirt and silt as those of sorrow are mollified by something positive.

The external situation is also portrayed in terms of the man's refusal to join the bandwagon and the response of the family and society towards the man. The obvious result of the man's negation of self-promoting greed is that he remains not only unsuccessful, but is also alienated from his family and the society. The situation is reflected in the poor opinion that his mother-in-law holds about him—useless, foolish and incapable of feeding his children. His wife, Oyo, also initially considers him a 'chichidodo' (43), a bird that eats worms but hates excrement. Having observed the glamorous life that Estella leads, she bluntly tells him: "Maybe you like this crawling that we do, but I am tired of it. I would like to have someone drive me where I want to go" (44). Later, the man informs Teacher that his wife had explained to him "step by step, that life was like a lot of roads: long roads, short roads, wide and narrow, steep and level, all sorts of roads" (58) and human beings were like "so many people driving their cars on all these roads" (59). Accidents would happen, she told him, but the fear of accidents would never keep men from driving and Joe Koomson had learned to drive. She asked the man what name he would give to people who were afraid to drive fast, or to drive at all.

The 'beautiful softness in the sweet direction of the gleam' (46) seems to hold everyone in its fold. This fatal attraction is reflected in "the forest of white men's names" the black men have adopted. The man, while walking on the street, realizes that there were very few 'black names of black men.' With such names as Mills-Hayford, Plange-Bannerman, Grantson, Fentengson and Binful, they were always 'trying mightily to be white' (126). Having seen 'Acromond' inscribed on a name-plate, the man wonders: "What Ghanaian name that could have been in the beginning, before its Civil Servant owner rushed to civilize it, giving it something like the sound of a master name?" (126)

The rot and decay that have crept into the roots of the society find their associative portrayals in the novel in a set of images different from those of regeneration and creation. The Atlantic-Caprice Hotel, with its grandeur and glassy shine epitomises the love and aspirations of the people. It is a twist of irony and human folly that this huge building, instead of 'attracting to itself all the massive anger of a people in pain,' in a situation of changed priorities, is drawing 'onto itself the love of a people hungry for just something such as this' (10).

If the static Atlantic-Caprice symbolizes one aspect of the 'gleam' that the people would like to possess, the 'drive' of Koomsons which enabled them to amass such fame and fortune and also their way of life represent another. Koomson's house is full of 'shiny things' (146). It was amazing for the man to see so much light in his house. The man comes to know that the name of their daughter is "Princess". He thinks aloud that it was a nickname to which Estella gives him a 'supercilious look' (148). Her pathological urge to imitate the Europeans is revealed in her remarks at the dinner hosted by the man: "This local beer . . . does not agree with my constitution" (131). She proudly informs the company that she had sent her sister to London where 'she's specializing in dressmaking' (148).

The man warns his family members against the purchasing of a boat, in which Koomson sees possibilities of furthering his own prosperity. But the family members would not pay heed to his advice. On the refusal of the man to sign the papers, his wife signs it, but ultimately it is Koomson who owns the boats. The man is so much disgusted with the hypocrisy of Koomson that he rejects the fish sent to him by the latter, thereby registering his protest against such greed and cheating.

Such an 'irresistible desire' in 'chasing after the gleam' (95), in the process of upward fortunes bears portents of a moribund culture. Teacher narrates the story of Aboligo the Frog and how he has shown a book of oddities in which they could see the peculiar picture of a 'man-child.' It was shown that the peculiar man-child completed the entire cycle of birth, growth and death in a short span of seven years. Just as the man-child is not destined to its full potential, the contemporary Ghanaian situation portends a life-negating and self-annihilating streak.

Yet another image that refelcts the prevailing situation is Plato's Cave. Teacher frequently narrates the story of the people living in the darkness of the cave. They cannot believe that brightness really exists. The person who goes outside the cave and experiences the light outside the world turns out to be a misfit among the worshippers of darkness. Groping in darkness, they dismiss him as mad and his outside experiences of brightness as untrue. In a society that is totally lacking in vision and direction, the man is forced to pass under its constant scrutiny which makes it 'terrifyingly plain that in these times honesty could only be a social vice' (51). Under these circumstances a person who scrupulously follows the party ideology is viewed as a man of 'very hostile form of selfishness, a very perverse selfishness' (52). Like the men in Plato's Cave, the society forces the man to review his position and throws open its options: 'When all around him the whole world never tired of saying there were only two types of men who took refuge in honesty—the cowards and fools. . . . Very often these days he was burdened with the hopeless, impotent feeling that he was not just one of these, but a hopeless combination of the two' (51). The novel, in these terms, becomes an extended metaphor of Plato's Cave. Margaret Folarin who interprets the novel in the light of this recurrent motif, says; "The cave image finally serves as a nucleus which holds together . . . positive meanings"[21] of the novel.

The internal and external factors have a cumulative impact on the mind of the man and his negation of corrupting influences gains a positive momentum, as the action of the novel progresses. This can be observed at two levels. In the first instance, his refusal to participate in the vicious game of manipulation and imitation becomes more solid as it reminds him of the centuries-old exploitation of the black people by the European colonizers. Secondly, the man's positive assertion is underlined in his relationship with

Teacher in a situation of changed roles.

The positive bent of the man's historical vision is portrayed in his realization that the contemporary situation is a perpetuation of the age-old exploitative methods, although by a different set of characters. For the man, the present situation is so startling that he is forced to comment:

> So this was the real gain. The only real gain. This was the thing for which poor men had fought and shouted. This was what it had come to: not that the whole thing might be overturned and ended, but that a few black men might be pushed closer to their masters, to eat some of the fat into their bellies too. That had been the entire end of it all. (126)

The man is amazed at the 'flabby softness' of the hand of Koomson when he shakes hands with him. The man wonders whether such 'Ideological hands' of revolutionaries 'leading others into bold sacrifices' should not have become 'even tougher than they were when their owner was hauling loads along the wharf?' (131) It reminds him of the age-old betrayal by the native cripples. He comments:

> And yet these were the socialists of Africa, fat, perfumed, soft with the ancestral softness of chiefs who had sold their people and are celestially happy with the fruits of the trade (131).

Teacher is not involved in these silent confrontations and inner conflicts since he has already withdrawn into his shell of isolation. When he was in a position of guiding the man, he appeared to be the alter ego of the man himself. All that is left of him now is depression and an irretrievable loss of faith in everything. He can only see all around death, the living death. He informs the man: "It is not a choice between life and death, but what kind of death we can bear, in the end. Have you not seen there is no salvation?" (56)

The man and Teacher find themselves in reversed roles. The man realizes the negative aspects of Teacher's attitude. There was a time when Teacher could speak about "the light and the shadow, the greatly beautiful things that could be and the starkly ugly thinngs that are." But now the man wonders, "whether this resignation does not make his naked friend infinitely smaller than he could be" (79). The man assumes the role of a judge, rather than a mere 'hearer.' His positive thinking negates the attitude of Teacher: "Why should there be such a need for shrinking the hoping self, and why must so much despair be so calmly embraced?" (79) The man is left all alone to chart out his own direction, since Teacher is no more a teacher, nor his alter ego.

The man has his roots firmly grounded in Ghana. He feels unhappy that there is a drift in the society and his helplessness to redeem it adds to his misery. His very non-participation in the national game of corruption and his refusal to fall in line with the bandwagon are in themselves the positive features of the novel. Henry Chakava, while commenting on the predicament of the man, says: "The man's determination to continue to live in the society and endure public disgrace, family abuse and mental conflict, without being defeated is the greatest sign of hope in the whole book."[22] In his determination to make his life yield a positive purpose, the man's struggle attains heroic proportions. The man continues his 'forward movement' (160), both physically and morally. We also learn that the natural walking as it is evidenced in his balancing act makes him feel 'very free and very light . . . enjoying his own movement.' (124)

A coup takes place in the country and Koomson finds himself on the run. But the irony is that the change of regimes following the coup is no positive indication of desirable outcome fulfilling the aspirations of the people. One cannot miss the foresight of the man when he opines that the change of the regime is nothing more than 'a change of embezzlers and a change of the hunters and the hunted' (162). The physical, psychological and moral degeneration of Koomson is tellingly brought out in the rapid transformation of his bearing. He cannot think of any safe place of shelter other than the man's house. He becomes a refuge at his place. The novelist juxtaposes the plight of the once powerful person with the relaxed condition of the man. This is how Armah is able to vindicate his moral vision, with the ultimate triumph of virtue. The darkness inside the house of the man is made more suffocating by the presence of Koomson, his fear, and his stench. His mouth had the 'rich stench of rotten menstrual blood' (161). It was overpowering, as if 'some corrosive gas, already half liquid, had filled the whole room.'

The degeneration of Koomson becomes complete as he was forced to escape through a latrine's hole, which he previously despised even to enter to attend nature's call. They take the help of a boat man to cross the shore. The boat man's voice helps to make another counter statement. There was still fear on the face of the boat man, but it was 'unmistakably the fear of one weak man in the presence of another just as weak' (173). Having accompanied Koomson near the other shore, the man jumps into the black water to come out with freshness. On his way back home, he observes an inscription in an oval shape on the back of a Mammy-Wagon which reads:

The Beautyful Ones
Are Not Yet Born

Ama Ata Aidoo, while commenting that "the details (in the novel) are incredible," says that "this type of purgative exposure, however painful it is, is absolutely necessary, depending upon whether or not one believes that truth as represented in writing can be in anyway effective in helping social change." She thinks that the novel's tone is a positive one. "What he [Armah] does proclaim is that he thinks of us. . . . Perhaps the beautiful ones, when they are born and let's pray it will be soon, will take care of everything and everybody once and for all time. The least we can do is wait."[23] The man realizes that the change of regime may not bring any real change in the structure of the society. Future does not behold all that bleakness either. The man is prepared to wait. When the future unfolds, it will not take the present models as its beautiful ones. This is summed up by the man himself:

> . . . he was not burdened with any hopes that new things, really new things, were as yet ready to come out. Someday in the long future a new life would maybe flower in the country, but when it came, it would not choose as its instruments the same people who had made a habit of killing new flowers. (159-60)

What holds good of this passage is also true of the novel and Armah's vision in general. It is the search for 'the things in the present' (160) that characterizes the man's burden. The novel, as mentioned by Folarin, deals with two aspects of life: It "accepts life as it may be observed at its very worst," but still unravels "much of the value of human existence."[24] The positive and progressive view of society is inherent in the negation of the former, which in itself provides a perfect launching pad for the inauguration of the 'beauty' and 'value' of human existence. Soyinka accurately strikes at this aspect in his response to the novel. Says he:

> The vision of *The Beautyful Ones* is perhaps no more than an aspiration, a pious hope symbolized in that final image of the novel—'a single flower, solitary, unexplainable, very beautiful,' in the centre of the inscription on the back of a Mammy-Wagon which reads: The Beautyful Ones Are Not Yet Born. This pessimistic suggestion bears the possibility of its own hopeful contradiction, an accurate summation of society only too well understood by Armah and expressed in the main action of the book through the solitary, beleagured representative of moral possibilities, the central character.[25]

If one chooses to ignore this aspect, the novel becomes a statement in "defeat, decay, shrinking and dwindling" as pointed out by Charles Nnolim.[26] Undoubtedly, Armah forces his readers to take note of the rot, ramshackle, the "shrinking and dwindling." At the same time, one cannot miss the unmistakable stamp of the writer's visionary ideal, an inner gaze and a passionate concern with the plight of his people. If the reality of the situation is frightening, the hope of the vision is equally encouraging. It is true that the change is no change in effect; the exploitation of the people is carried on in another name and another form. The independence is wasted in the process, along with inspiration which it has brought in its wake. The people are caught irredeemably in a vicious circle of manipulation and hopelessness. It is equally true that the revolutionary conditions do not exist and yet, the margin for hope is not totally lost, first indicated in the evocative title itself, the "not yet" implying possibilities of the beautiful ones of future. The man's stubborn refusal to participate in the all round phenomenon of 'cutting corners, and eating the fruits of fraud' (95) is a positive feature of the novel.

The motif of feminine principle is introduced in the novel although in a subdued manner. The man's dogged refusal to abandon his principles and his dream of a better society finds its reward, with his wife sharing his natural movement of walking. Robert Fraser argues that his marriage with Oyo is the result of an 'amorous misadventure'[27] for which he has not stopped feeling sorry. But a close reading of the novel reveals that the man looks to Oyo for inspiration and approval and feels himself lost when he can no longer reach her. The man's denial of gleam is creative, for it opens the way for the beautiful ones, the course of which his wife has already endorsed by saying 'I am glad you never became like him' (165).

NOTES

1. Ayi Kwei Armah, *The Beautyful Ones Are Not Yet Born* (Boston: Houghton Mifflin, 1968; London: Heinemann Educational Books, 1969). All page references are to the Heinemann edition.
2. Chinua Achebe, 'Africa and Her writers,' *Morning Yet on Creation Day* (London: Heinemann, 1975), p. 25.
3. Eldred Durosimi Jones, in his review of *The Beautyful Ones Are Not Yet Born, African Literature Today* (London: Heinemann), No. 3, p. 55.
4. *Ibid.*, p. 56.
5. Charles E. Nnolim, "Dialectic as Form: Pejorism in the Novels of Armah," *African Literature Today*, No. 10 (1979), p. 210.
6. Emmanuel Obiechina, review in *Okike* (Nigeria, NSUKKA, April 1971), p. 49.
7. Shatto Arthur Gakwandi, *The Novel and Contemporary Experience in Africa* (London: Heinemann, 1977), p. 91.
8. Lewis Nkosi, *Tasks and Masks* (London: Longman Group, 1981), p. 67.
9. *Ibid.*
10. O.R. Dathorne, *African Literature in the Twentieth Century* (Minneapolis: University of Minnesota Press, 1974), p. 105.
11. Robert Fraser, *The Novels of Ayi Kwei Armah* (London: Heinemann,

1980), pp. 25-26.

12. Neil Lazarus, "Pessimism of the Intellect, Optimism of the Will: A Reading of Ayi Kwei Armah's *The Beautyful Ones Are Not Yet Born*," *Research in African Literatures*, Vol. 18, No. 2 (1987), p. 137.
13. Rand Bishop, "The Beautyful Ones Are Born: Armah's First Five Novels," *World Literature Written in English*, Vol. 21, No. 3 (Autumn 1982), p. 532.
14. Chinua Achebe, in an interview with Kalu Ogbaa, *Research in African Literatures*, Vol. 12, No. 1 (Spring 1981), pp. 4-5.
15. Frantz Fanon, *The Wretched of the Earth* (London: Penguin Books, 1967), p. 120.
16. Ayi Kwei Armah, "African Socialism: Utopian or Scientific?," *Presence Africaine*, No. 64 (1967), p. 28.
17. Ama Ata Aidoo, 'No Saviors,' *African Writers on African Writing* (Essays), ed. G.D. Killam (London: Heinemann, 1973), p. 14.
18. As quoted by Neil Lazarus, pp. 139-40.
19. Kolawole Ogungbesan, "Symbol and Meaning in *The Beautyful Ones Are Not Yet Born,*" *African Literature Today*, No. 7 (1975), p. 93.
20. Neil Lazarus, p. 162.
21. Margaret Folarin, "An Additional Comment on Ayi Kwei Armah's *The Beautyful Ones Are Not Yet Born*," *African Literature Today*, Vol. 5 (1971), p. 122.
22. Henry Chakava, "Ayi Kwei Armah and a Commonwealth of Souls," *Standpoints on African Literature: A Critical Anthology*, ed. C. Wanjala (Nairobi: East African Literature Bureau, 1973), p. 202.
23. Ama Ata Aidoo, p. 18.
24. Margaret Folarin, p. 128.
25. Wole Soyinka, *Myth, Literature and the African World* (Cambridge: Cambridge University Press, 1976), p. 116.
26. Charles E. Nnolim, "Dialectic as Form: Pejorism in the Novels of Armah," *African Literature Today*, No. 10 (1987), p. 207.
27. Robert Fraser, p. 16.

In Search of Wholeness:
Fragments

Armah's second novel *Fragments*[1] was first published in America in 1970. Four years later, it was published in England and finally made its way to Africa. Although there are thirteen chapters in the novel, each with a sub-title of its own, it does not in itself become fragmented. On the other hand, the episodic narration and the cinematic techniques of spotlight and flashback coupled with the tone of mythical past add a new dimension to the tempo of narration. The novel, as a whole, presents a unified picture prompting Robert Fraser to comment that "Armah's second novel is probably his most unified, structurally as well as thematically."[2]

The complexity of the theme and structure of the novel requires a careful analysis. Rand Bishop confesses that the first reading of the novel disappointed him but says subsequent readings helped him "appreciate the care and precision that went into the construction"[3] of the novel. Many critics are of the opinion that *Fragments* is essentially a representation of the themes of *The Beautyful Ones Are Not Yet Born*. While it is true that the novel presents characters that are similar to *The Beautyful Ones Are Not Yet Born* in certain respects, it is much more than the first novel in its theme and structure. Gerald Moore concedes that the novel "will eventually establish itself as superior to *The Beautyful Ones* in quality, profoundity and originality."[4]

The old-world wisdom of Naana, the blind grandmother of the protagonist, underlines the opening and closing chapters of the novel providing a mythical experience. The significance of the title of the novel and its structural patterns are reflected in the thinking of Naana in the last chapter:

> The larger meaning which lent sense to every small thing and every momentary happening years and years ago has shattered into a thousand and thirty useless pieces. Things have

> passed which I have never seen whole, only broken and twisted against themselves. What remains of my days will be filled with broken things. (280)

This leads to the erroneous interpretation of the novel in religious terms. Robert Fraser says that 'the thirty pieces' of 'a thousand and thirty useless pieces' symbolize Juda's betrayal of Jesus.[5] His far-fetched interpretation of the novel in religious terms does not hold good in this context. The novel achieves its wholeness not by its religious implications, but through the concerns of the individuals confronted with a demanding family and a fragmented society. Inherent in this observation is one of the justifiable approaches to the novel. The impact of the shattering of 'the larger meaning' of the social order and moral vision is felt by individuals who wish to restore order and a sense of justice. This process often leads to conflicts from within and without. This also results in violence particularly when the society and its miniature representation, family, takes an unsympathetic view of the individuals' efforts to live a meaningful existence. This is demonstrated in the novel through the characters of Baako, his grandmother, Naana, and his Puerto Rican psychiatrist-girl friend, Juana.

It is significant to note that the fragmentation is portrayed in internal and external terms. The society is fragmented in the absence of a just social order and valid ideology. However, like the man in *The Beautyful Ores Are Not Yet Born*, Naana and her spiritual companion, Baako, struggle to preserve their cherished values swimming against the tide. Consequently, they become victims of conflicting tendencies within, as exemplified in Baako's occasional nervous breakdown and Naana's death-wish. Naana, for instance, in the last chapter, is shattered because of violence in many forms which she feels could have been avoided. She contemplates death as a way out of this sordid situation:

> The time has come. What lies outside me is ready for me, and I too am ready to go. Such inward readiness to go does not come if this world here has room and use for us. When there is no use the spirit in us yearns for the world of other spirits themselves hope and wait for the new one coming.

> Here I have come the remnant of something that passed by and was immediately forgotten; the fruits that fell from my own entrails are looking hard for ways to push me into the earth deeper than where my navel is buried and to stamp the ground above me smooth with their hasty soles. (278)

The narrative of *Fragments* is exposed through Naana's encompassing vision. In her blindness, she is a visionary. The incantatory tone of Naana in the first chapter of the novel serves as a prologue followed by the point of view of Juana. Naana's thoughtful commentary on the life that has been lived and its future portents in the last chapter are like the epilogue which, in turn, is preceded by Juana's pragmatic vision. Both of them represent the significance of feminine principle, lending structural as well as thematic coherence to the novel. The opening passage of the novel sets the theme in earnest:

> Each thing that goes away returns and nothing in the end is lost. The great friend throws all things apart and brings all things together again. That is the way everything goes and turns round. That is how all living things come back after long absences, and in the whole great world all things are living things. All that goes returns. He will return. (1)

Baako, a young man of twenty six, is expected to return home after a five year stay in New York, where he did a course in creative writing. He arrives unannounced, having cut short his stay in Paris. His return does not pave the way for a cosy future either for him or for the family, as Naana initially imagined. He refuses to fulfil the role of a 'been-to' on his return. A 'been-to' is expected to bring fortunes to the family and elevate its standing in the social echelons and hence is looked upon as a demi-god and offered special treatment by the society. This is portrayed through the character of Brempong whom the family and the society adulate on his return.

Baako's family looks upto him as an Osagyefo, the saviour of the family's fortunes. His mother, Efua, greets him with high expectations on his arrival. She expectantly enquires about the car, which, she thought, might be in transit. Baako remembers in a flashback how his family members and the near ones gathered to celebrate the occasion of his arrival. He wonders why all those 'fripperies' were arranged and remembers as having told them bluntly that there was nothing to celebrate. He also remembers how his mother hoped that he would complete the unfinished house which she had undertaken keeping in view the status of a 'been-to.' The disillusioned mother tells him:

> We come to walls in life, all the time. If we try to break them down we destroy ourselves. I was wanting you to break down and see the world here, before I saw you yourself were a wall. (253)

Baako chooses to serve his society as a script writer for Ghanavision (the state television). This serves a two-fold purpose: As a script writer, he hopes to fulfil his creative urges lending relevance to his studies in America. He says: "I was thinking of it as a way of making my life mean something to me" (114). Besides, this vocation enables him to reach out to the illiterate masses. Baako, who pinned a lot of hopes on the Ghanavision is very soon disillusioned as it became synonymous with the corrupt regime of the state. It also became the mouth-piece of the Head of State. The slavish sycophancy is only a mask to cover up their inability to formulate any new and constructive ideas. Baako's scripts are rejected and even his constructive ideas are negatived.

Baako resigns his job and consigns all his scripts to flames. Looked upon as a misfit by the family and society, he takes to writing about men, matters and contemporary situation. For the family, and for its 'cargo mentality,' always on the look-out for a saviour, Baako becomes no more than a mad person with all his writings on something it could not comprehend. In spite of his protests, he is forcibly confined to an asylum, accentuating the process of his nervous breakdown.

Naana is a silent witness to the needless violence perpetrated in many forms. In her epilogue-like commentary in the last chapter, we realize that her basic individual position of loneliness has not changed so much as the situation around her. Her hopeful waiting and wishful thinking as discernible in the first chapter have not entirely gone unrewarded. But what has taken place later is something unexpected. In the last chapter, Naana recaptures in her brooding moments, what has happened:

> The return of this one traveler had held out so much of good hope. But there were those left behind who had their dreams and put them on the shoulders of the traveler returned, heavy dreams and hopes filled with the mass of things here and of this time. And another spirit has already found its death in the hot wet embrace of people who have forgotten that fruit is not a gathered gift of the instant but seed hidden in the earth and tended and waited for and allowed to grow—so busy have they become in their reaching new things and newer ways to consume them. (282-83)

The 'traveler' referred to in the above passage is Baako who becomes a victim of the materialist aspirations of the family which are 'filled with the mass of things here and of this time' only. 'Another spirit' mentioned in the passage is a reference to the newborn child of Araba. Baako saves both his sister and the child by giving his blood. The family members have forgotten that the child is like a fruit—a 'seed hidden in the earth and tended and waited for and allowed to grow.' The child also falls a victim to the materialist schemes of the family members in their greed to collect gifts, since they consider it to be 'a gathered gift of the instant.' They are thus concerned with the immediate present to the exclusion of past and future.

The novel, as such, is as much a story of the child as about Baako. The child image haunts the consciousness of the principal characters in the novel and serves as a nucleus that holds the meanings of the novel together. It is also an extended metaphor, signifying the plight of Baako. Naana identifies herself with the child and tells Nananom, the mythical past and the world of the ancestors, of 'those who have gone before': "A new child coming back to you" (286). She wonders why so much violence is perpetuated: "For what purpose do you throw us such blinding sweetness when our aim is death?" (286)

Juana provides a silver lining in this sordid drama of greed and spiritual mutation. She shares the positive vision of Naana and Baako. In a society that is full of 'heavy dreams of things,' Juana craves for the soothing human touch, 'the hunger for which continued in her in spite of everything' (19). This sustained search for a meaning in their surroundings eventually unites Baako and Juana. A psychiatrist that Juana is, she tries to heal Baako's physical and psychological wounds. He feels lonely and miserable when she is not around. Juana too hopefully waits for Baako's recovery, just as Naana waited for his safe return in the opening pages of the novel. Thus, the opening and concluding passages of the novel converge on the same idea:

> All that goes returns. He will return. (1)

II

In the encompassing vision of Naana, Baako and Juana together become her interpreters. She paves initially the way for Baako's return and then laments that all hopes have been shattered. It is one of the ironies in the novel that without eyes she sees more than others. But endowed with voice and speaking ability, she speaks little: "If I see things unseen by those who have eyes, why should my wisest speech not be silence?" (3) She survives to see the return of Baako, her spiritual companion, and the birth of a new child in the family. But when they are driven to a state of breakdown—both in mental and physical terms—she thinks of her own death.

The return of 'the traveler' is marked by hope and expectancy. Naana invokes the wisdom of those gone before to ensure the success of Baako's travel. She remembers Baako's departure and foretells his imminent return. Her prayers bear an ample testimony to her psychological union with the mythical past:

> Your blessings
> Your help
> In this life you have left us to fight alone.
> With your wisdom
> Let him go,
> Let him come. (8-9)

On his return, Baako finds himself entangled in a tricky situation. He knows that he is not cut out for the role of a 'been-to' which his family expects of him. He cannot expose himself to the general trend of greed and easy gain. He wants to serve his society in his artistic vocation, but steeped as it is in hypocrisy, it also views his attempts with suspicion. This is because the society judges the achievement of an individual from the standpoint of family, its microcosm. In the context of corruption and moral depravity, Baako's pragmatic thinking appears to be idealistic. Baako's attempt at reconciliation between the familial aspirations and societal demands has been summed up by Juana at the end in terms of the cargo-cult. She tells Ocran:

> It can be a terrifying conflict, if you see the need to help the relation, though, and also to do something useful in a larger sense. There are two communities, really, and they don't coincide. It's not easy to work out priorities. (273)

The inner conflict in Baako, the 'been-to,' is set forth and pointedly referred to when he meets one Mr. Brempong, another 'been-to,' on his way back home. It also serves as a point of contrast and counterstatement. He is 'a man of the people' in the sense that he feels the pulse of the people and, unlike Baako, acts accordingly. He bears close resemblances to Koomson in *The Beautyful Ones Are Not Yet Born.* He enjoys a sense of belonging with his family. The society also adulates him for the same material prosperity which he tries to acquire at its cost. He learns that Baako is returning home empty-handed, save for a type-writer and a guitar for his personal use. He tells Baako, although belatedly, what is expected of a 'been-to': "You just have to know what to look for when you get a chance to go abroad. Otherwise, you come back empty-handed like a fool, and all the time you spent is a waste, useless." (66)

Brempong plays a 'dizzy game' (88) in order to receive respect from his family and community. But for Baako, it is a 'desperate inflated game' (88). The contrast between their two worlds is strikingly brought out in the grand reception offered to Brempong on his arrival at Accra airport. He offers his relatives and friends what they need and gets what he wants. It is mutual and reciprocal. Brempong finds in the game 'an easy potency,' in which he has nothing original to show, nor any eagerness 'to create' (88). The waiting crowd goes into raptures at his very sight. His sister's ridiculous eulogies show how the entire community treats him as a demi-god. On his part, Brempong appears to be a man caught 'happily in the center of his crowd like a man who had looked so long to just some such beautiful sort of trap' (87-88).

Baako wonders at the greed and hypocrisy of the people around Brempong and realizes that the 'show was designed to hide impotence' (89). For him, it was like an invitation into a pretended world in which everything is 'happily given, happily taken, so completely accepted that there had hardly been any of the pretenders to whom it could have seemed unreal' (88). He warns himself that 'he would have to be the careful one' (89). At the same time the ceremony accentuates his loneliness and a sense of fear invades him at the thought of facing his family members. While cautioning himself repeatedly that he would have to be careful he examines his own changing self: 'impotent sometimes, growing, sometimes strong, confused, often weak, changing, many things by turns' (93).

The impending doom of the sensitive individual in the context of spiritual mutation is forewarned through a series of cinematic episodes, flashbacks and superimposition. The outdooring ceremony of the child is an extended metaphor which lends meaning to the overlapping consciousness of Baako and Naana. Soon after Baako's return, he saves the life of his sister, Araba, who gives birth to a premature baby. He gives his blood in order to save both the mother and the child. Araba had five miscarriages earlier, and she acknowledges that Baako's arrival augured well for her and says: "Now see it is such a good thing, your coming" (120). But the happiness was short-lived. Araba and her mother, Efua, plan to advance the date of outdooring ceremony to the fifth day of the baby's 'homecoming' from the normal eighth day. They believe that the ceremony held more than a few days after payday would be 'useless.' Baako tries to stop them by asking, "Are you so pressed you have to make money out of the child?" (126) Naana also feels that the child is still in the 'keeping' of the spirits and they should not hurry 'dragging him out into this world for eyes in heads that have eaten flesh to gape at' (138). She is, however, even more helpless than Baako in preventing them from proceeding with their ritual. She knows that what they are planning is not good to the child. That is why she says: "You know the child is only a traveler between the world of spirits and this one of heavy flesh. His birth can be a good beginning, and he may find his body and this world around it a home where he wants to stay. But for this he must be protected. Or he will run screaming back, fleeing the horrors prepared for him up there." (139)

Baako's warning and Naana's sense of foreboding come true when the child dies during the ceremony itself. Naana analyses the problem more clearly and tries to posit it in the larger perspective. For her, the killing of the child is the result of their loss of faith in the 'wisdom of those gone before' (284) but wonders 'what new power has made them forget that a child too soon exposed is bound to die?' She feels that the baby was a sacrifice they offered to a new god, a cardinal failing from a historical point of view. They have been exhibiting this all the way. The new god they have found is much like the white destroyers who began the long destruction of 'our people.' The 'great haste to consume things we have taken no care nor trouble to produce' (284) must be viewed in this larger historical perspective.

Even before the outdooring ceremony, the motif of death has been introduced. Baako and Araba's husband, Bukari, go to a bar where they see a man drinking excessively and weeping over the death of his mother. As soon as Baako mentions that the child was prematurely born and special care had to be taken, he hears the noise of splintering glass beside him. Even from the loud speaker they hear the music of death:

> Tomarrow I'll begone,
>
> Bluebottle flies swarming over me. . . .

On the day of the ceremony itself, an eerie feeling of doom prevails in the house. They have brought a ram to be killed and eaten in celebration of the child's entry into the outer world: "in a moment the back of the yard was filled with the rising smoke and the smell of burning hair and flesh, and the hunchback added the sharp screech of metal on metal as he sharpened other knives for the cutting he would have to do." (137)

It is significant to note that the family in its haste 'to consume things,' severes its links with past, present and future. But Naana in her visionary thinking and Baako in his vocation are creators. Naana identifies herself with Baako when she says: "Happy event if in his future there is yet something hidden that will reveal itself with time, though that will be long after I'am dead" (284). Baako, in turn, identifies himself with the child whom he had saved by donating his blood: "He looked past at the baby on the bed. Babyhood, infancy, going to school . . . the thought of a person having to go through the whole cycle again brought back his nausea" (122) Naana herself says that the child belonged to him: 'The child is yours to look after. . . . The blood that flows in Araba is yours, Baako, and the child is yours also if it is hers' (139-40). Like the child itself, his arrival is unexpected and the source of their strength is life-giving principle. Again like 'the child travelor,' Baako is offered as a sacrifice to the 'new god.'

Baako's attempts at finding a meaningful existence by relating himself to the larger society in his artistic vocation are also thwarted. The positive aspect of Baako's thinking is stressed in his wish to serve the community through his vocation. He thus provides a link to his communal past and traditional ethos. But Baako's sensibility suffers a serious setback when even the society views his attempts with undue hostility. The sterility that has affected the society is experienced not merely by Baako but by many others. Everybody in the city seems to be aware of it. When Baako looks at the time-table in a bus-stop, a woman laughs at him. The taxi-driver who takes Araba to the hospital frowns, 'Ghana life sweet oh.' To his dismay, he learns that the best medical care and facilities are provided exclusively for V.I.Ps in Government hospitals. When Baako tells his art-teacher that he had sent his papers to the Ministry three weeks ago, Ocran mutters: "Nothing works in this country. What can you expect? The place is run by this so-called elite of pompous asses trained to do nothing" (116). Even the husband-wife relations are strained as Araba says that she uses her 'secret weapon' to make her husband yield to her way. Juana also feels the need for flight which urges her to leave the 'whole aborted town' just to get out of the nauseating thought that she was here in 'another defeated and defeating place' (17). But she reassures herself that some day 'the deadly seriousness people here invested in these external things' would crack up and let their 'inner worth' come out.

Armah's narrative technique of flashbacks and cinematic projection of a series of episodes is very significant in shedding light on the details. It also serves a two-fold purpose: On the one hand, it becomes an extended metaphor for the main theme of the novel. At the same time, it provides an insight into the thinking process of the characters. For instance, the first of these episodes is presented from the point of view of Juana in the second chapter named 'Edin.' It is also an extended metaphor, preparing the ground for Baako's return. The killing of the dog is narrated in slow motion technique and in elaborate terms. The spotlight is focussed on the incident, and it brings out the reactions of the observer as well.

Juana stops at the Kalifonia Moon Beam cafe where she finds a huge crowd of people. The focus of attention is the scene of violence being unleashed against a helpless dog by the crowd. Against this unjustifiable violence could be heard a lone, feeble voice of a boy imploring the crowd not to kill his dog. But his is a cry in the wilderness. For Juana, the scene of violence is diabolic and she is horrified at the sight of a man with 'a manic shine with far more burn than that possessing any of the others' (27) in his eyes. The physical deformity of the man inevitably prompted him to exhibit his masculinity in an act that opens up a psychological vent for his pent-up feelings. He moves fast and strikes first. The gory scene of violence and the sense of satisfaction at having emerged a victor releases 'something that had stayed locked up and poisoned the masculinity of his days' (29). The episode is an indication of what is in store for Baako after his return. He is forewarned that if he is unable to strike a rapport between the demands of his community and his inner self, the danger of being dubbed insane always looms large. As the action of the novel is unfolded, we come to know that in the process of the society literally hunting down Baako, the helpless Naana, like the boy, remains a silent spectator.

Juana also realizes that Baako does not exactly fit into the scheme of things. She feels that 'a situation and a place' like this, 'could so easily turn his lucidity into some vertiginous disease' unless he took great care or 'found survival by shedding this painful ability to see so clearly' (143). In a flashback she remembers Skido, the lorry driver who was anxious to get his food loads across the Yeji ferry to the market. He has already waited for three days and is afraid that the food stuffs may get rotten. He takes up the issue with the authorities. But his plea goes unheeded. In the ensuing rush that follows, his lorry gets overturned resulting in his death. The Chief Engineer takes the news from Baako casually and does not show any inclination to take preventive measures to avoid recurrence of such fatal accidents. Armah's satire is directed against the Ghanaian officials who, far from being innovative, are superficial and self-centred. These episodes are important since the reasons for Baako's failure abound in them.

Baako's commitment to a life-restoring principle makes him stand apart from a people who are bereft of ideals. His sensibility is informed and strengthened by his awareness of the role of a creative writer in the society which is in its period of transition. He expects himself and others in the vocation to serve the community, but should not prosper at its cost. Baako sees the fulfilment of his wishes of serving the society in his role as a script writer for Ghanavision. He thinks that as an artistic opportunity 'the chance of doing film scripts for an illiterate audience would be superior to writing.' It would be a matter of images, not words. This also enables him to reach out to the illiterate masses: "it's a much clearer way of saying things to people here."

Armah uses the technique of deflation to drive home the point that Baako's thinking is out of place in the given context. The Principal Secretary of the Ministry bluntly advises Baako: "If you come back thinking you can make things work in any smooth, efficient way, you'll just get a complete waste of time. It's not worth bothering about." With an uncanny sense of foreboding, he tells Ocran what really works in the country: "Unfortunately . . . the young man will also be finding out that making a go of life means forgetting all the beautiful stuff they teach in the classroom" (118).

Baako later finds, much to his chagrin, the words of the Secretary coming true with frightening clarity. What he finds at the Ghanavision is a total negation of purposeful thinking. Asante-Smith, the Director of Ghanavision and his other colleagues are incapable of anything that is creative and their commitment is to the powers-that-be. The degenerated set-up is tellingly brought out in the silly yet, dehumanizing scuffle following the distribution of television sets. Two persons from Technicians' chamber resort to physical violence for a leftover set. The stronger of the two knocks down the smaller man and picks up the set and strides confidently forward. But the fallen man, in an unexpected movement, hurls a stone with hard force at the television set. The brand new set is broken in the process. Thus the dog, the child and the inanimate television set become the targets of avoidable violence.

Baako's commitment to his society and his artistic vocation are out of tune with a people who are known for their creative impotence. At the production meeting, Baako presents his script about slavery entitled 'The Root' but Asante-Smith dismisses the treatment with a small yawn: "Look, we're a free, independent people. We're engaged in a gigantic task of nation-building. We have inherited a glorious culture, and that's what we're here to deal with" (209). Baako presents another treatment, 'The Brand', about survival. But the Director, interested as he is in the process of 'nation-building' by turning his cameras on the head of state, comments on Baako: "I know what the trouble is with you. You're too abstract in your approach to our work. For instance, what you've just said has nothing to do with our people's culture—all this slavery, survival, the brand" (209).

Baako's treatment of the questions of slavery and survival in his scripts assumes significance in that they raise fundemental questions over the tampering of the newly-acquired independence and hard-fought struggle against colonialism. For instance, in 'The Brand,' there is a ladder from a weak circle symbolizing servitude to a strong square representing independence, as shown in the long shot. The hero, dim and abstract, is not to be shown in the close-up. He climbs the ladder, made up of the shoulders of inhabitants of the circle, the oppressed, and reiterates his promise that he will liberate the others once he has climbed on. But the old man's cynical warning that the hot promises are worth nothing comes true. The hero clings to the square, unwilling to come back: "THE CLIMB ITSELF, THE PROCESS OF GETTING TO THE SQUARE, HAS INJECTED INTO HIS BEING AN ADDICTION TO WAYS AND HABITS DIAMETRICALLY OPPOSED TO THE LIBERATOR'S CAREER" (210) (capitals original).

Other characters include a weeping woman who is ignored by everybody. She firmly says that the square is there not to absorb the circle. There is the thinker, the intellectual who, in 'flashes of manic eloquence,' preaches his favourite theme of defeating the square with the force of the square itself. The script is a startling revelation of the African reality which is marked by total indifference of the leaders towards the plight of the masses with whose participation they have climbed up the ladder.

In his loneliness and general gloominess, Baako finds a source of strength and vitality in the company of Juana. When Baako comes to her as a patient, Juana feels a 'comforting pigeonholing reflex,' although she tries to take refuge in the thought of being a doctor, searching 'for the ease of dealing with a patient' (143). As a sensitive individual, Juana finds him much closer to her own inner self and she cannot reject his offer of friendship. She understands his 'painful ability to see so clearly' and this understanding gets reinforced through the scenes of love-making on the beach and in the sea. As Gerald Moore remarks: "It is with Juana that he also experiences some moments of overlapping vision and those blinding moments of sensual joy which illuminate some of the tenderest and most explicit scenes of love making to be found in African literature."[6]

Baako and Juana once observe a boy singing songs continuously on the beach, while the fishermen are engaged in work. Although the fishermen do not seem to be aware of it, the boy, in his act of singing, provides rhythm and inspiration to the elders. When Juana says that Baako had eyes only for the little boy, he replies: "The boy, he was giving those men something they didn't have" (185). The comment reveals what Baako himself is striving for. The boy, like Baako, is engaged in creative work. But the people around them are insensitive to their inspiring and creative capabilities. What Baako is struggling against will come into light from his own point of view if we compare the above comment with his observation made in his discussion with Juana on another occasion. In his first meeting with Juana, she observes that he is going against a general current. He replies that it is not merely a current and says: "As a matter of fact it's beginning to look like a cataract to me" (148). When Juana asks why he preferred the word—'cataract'—to 'waterfall' he simply says that he is not a very dramatic person. For him, the term 'cataract' rather than any other describes the essence of the force he is trying to face upto. The influence of this cataract can be traced to the destructive capabilities of their colonial masters of the recent history. In *Two Thousand Seasons* Armah tellingly makes use of the word while referring to the white enslavers:

> Giver of life, spring whose water now pours down destruction's road a rushing cataract, your future is destruction. Your present a giving, giving into a void with no return. Your flow knows no regeneration.[7]

In *The Beautyful Ones Are Not Yet Born*, the man turns to Teacher and his family for inspiration. In *Fragments*, Juana provides moments of comfort and solace to Baako. Both of them attend an art-session in which Akosua-Russell, president of the Writers' Workshop and Ford Foundation Money, and other members exhibit hypocrisy and undisguised snobbery. Baako and Juana are stunned by the creative impotence of the President and some of the members. The episode accentuates their sense of isolation. Juana thus, understands Baako's predicament and shares his private moments of joy, sorrow and loneliness. But the feminine principle as demonstrated by Juana underlines man-woman relationship, the ramifications of which go beyond their loneliness. After their first act of love-making on the beach, Baako narrates the myth of "Mame Water and the Musician" according to which the lonely musician goes to the beach playing his instrument. The beautiful goddess of Mame Water emerges from the water and they make love. She leaves him to go back to the sea, and they meet at long, fixed intervals. The musician cannot bear separation. However, it brings the best out of him and he sings as he has never done before. In this myth of "Mame Water," the absence of the goddess makes him reach the zenith of his creative capabilities. But in his own life, Baako crumbles under pressure in the absence of Juana.

Baako's resignation for his job precipitates the conflict between the community and his struggling self. His failure to register success in a corrupt and degenerated society turns him into a writer. As a sensitive man and perceptive writer, he looks upon his family as an encumbrance and interprets it in terms of Melanesian cargo mythology. He compares the expectations of the family with the 'ritual games' played by the people in Melanesia:

> CARGO MENTALITY. The expectancy, the waiting for bounty dropping from the sky through benign intercession of dead ancestors, the beneficent ghosts. Out there in ancestral territory beyond the cemetery the goods are available in abundance, no doubt at all about that in Melanesian cargo mythology (228).

For the family, his writings become a sure sign of madness. The family members insist on taking him to a hospital. But Baako refuses to be taken to the asylum for treatment. The family members chase him, and a mob joins the race. It is ironical that Araba whom he had saved by donating blood feels compelled to direct the mob to tie him up with ropes. The litany of sorrow the people express and the sense of sympathy they show for him are in reality only 'strangely twisted truths and unaccountable lies, all flowing together in a stream he could do nothing to stop' (247). The contrast between the prosperity of Brempong and the plight of Baako is tellingly brought out in the scene of stone-throwing. Baako, in order to escape the fury of surging crowds, waves at the passing cars. In one of the cars he sees Brempong and hopefully shouts his name but it remains a cry in wilderness as the car whizzes past him. Subsequently he faces the wrath of the surging crowd. He is tied up with ropes and forcibly admitted into a hospital.

Armah's ability to scrupulously survey the reality by throwing the searchlight on the minute details and his technique of presenting the action through a series of flashbacks and episodes as evidenced in the novel are breathtaking. The familial aspirations and expectations are diligently brought out in the outdooring ceremony of the child and pointedly referred to in the tumultuous welcome reserved for the likes of Brempong. The societal fragmentation and spiritual mutation are stunningly portrayed in the killing of dog and the violent death of Skido. The hypocrisy of the social order is depicted in the self-projection of the authorities at Ghanavision and the meaningless exercises carried out at the Writers' Workshop in the name of training youngsters in creative writing. Both the factors—familial and societal—converge on in the end to precipitate the crisis in Baako's life.

The forcible confinement of Baako to the asylum is the culmination of all forces working against the individual's sensibility. The dialogue between Baako and Ocran in the hospital brings out the precarious nature of Baako's conflicts. Ocran says:

> "You know. Don't stop thinking, Onipa. You have a good mind; don't be afraid to use it. Stop thinking you've done people wrong. Nobody cares, anyway. If these people had your talent, they wouldn't want to be that way. They wouldn't need to."
>
> "They're useful."
>
> "If that's all the usefulness you can think of. We all have relatives who want us to be like your Brempong—get them things that shout they're rich, they're powerful. But you don't have time for that nonsense. The country's full of people dying to look down on everybody else" (274).

When Ocran and Juana come out of the hospital, Juana tells him: "Salvation is such an empty thing when you're alone" (276). Ocran replies: "You don't find it in the marketplace. You have to be alone to find what's in you."

The seemingly irreconcilable positions adopted by Juana and Ocran provide a clue to the conflicts in Baako. In this bleak picture and the sordid drama presented in the novel, the writer's visionary ideal is filtered through the overlapping consciousness of Naana, Baako and Juana. Together, they offer a connectedness between past, present and future. Naana, for instance, implores the surging crowds to spare Baako from such inhuman treatment.

She says: "What have you done to him? What has Baako done to you? Where is he?" (248) Baako belongs to her spiritually, but like the boy in the initial pages of the novel, she is pushed back in the scrimmage. The writer's penetrating vision upholds wholeness and connectedness as it attemps to carefully posit the inner meaning in a larger historical perspective through the principle of feminine fertility. Juana bears portents of hope. Although she is pained by the 'old slave castle which had now become the proud seat of the new rulers, the blind children of slavery themselves,' (44) she also realizes that 'the burning of old frames and the shedding of cruel blood would not be against the making of another world' (45). She embodies the youthful vigour which prompted her to think that 'if the beautiful colors were mixed with the red of blood and the sulfrous yellow of flames, that was in no way a reason to run from the dream' (45).

The human touch provided by Juana at the hospital to Baako's bruised psyche also brings portents of hope and recovery, and as she took his hand and held it, 'a fullness of affection she had been unable to let out in words broke through and took complete possession of her' (272). Baako also feels it and moves closer to her as 'the resistance that had been so strong in his words was gone, and his body next to hers felt totally willing. He was crying.' She invites him to her place when he is discharged from the hospital. At the end of the novel, she is busy preparing the unused room for Baako.

Armah's understanding of the capacity of women for creativity and destruction is evident in the novel. V.U. Ola, while commenting on the principle of feminine fertility in the novels of Armah maintains thus:

> Among African writers, Armah and Ngugi are the two who have demonstrated the greatest insight and sensitivity as well as rare ability to artistically portray the problems and fears of the African woman and to delve imaginatively deep into the wells of her being. Armah, however, more than Ngugi towers above the rest in capturing the enigmatic combination of good and evil in her nature.[8]

In *Fragments* Naana and Juana partake in the process of healing and creation whereas Araba and Efua are on the destructive side. But the stress is always on the woman as the fountain-head of love, inspiration and fertility in the process of self-discovery.

NOTES

1. Ayi Kwei Armah, *Fragments* (Boston: Houghton Mifflin, 1970; London: Heinemann Educational Books, 1974; Nairobi: East African Publishing House, 1974). Page references are to the Heinemann edition.
2. Robert Fraser, *The Novels of Ayi Kwei Armah* (London: Heinemann, 1980), p. 30.
3. Rand Bishop, "The Beautyful Ones Are Born: Armah's First Five Novels," *WLWE*, Vol. 21, No. 3 (Autumn 1982), p. 532.
4. Gerald Moore, "Armah's Second Novel," *The Journal of Commonwealth Literature*, Vol. IX, No. 11 (August 1974), p. 69.
5. Robert Fraser, *The Novels of Ayi Kwei Armah* (London: Heinemann, 1980), p. 30.
6. Gerald Moore, p. 70.
7. Ayi Kwei Armah, *Two Thousand Seasons* (London: Heinemann, 1979), Prologue xii.
8. V.U. Ola, "The Feminine Principle and the Search for Wholeness in *The Healers*," *UFAHAMU*, Vol. XIV, No. 3 (1985), pp. 73-74.

Connecting Centre:
Why Are We So Blest?

Ayi Kwei Armah's third novel, *Why Are We So Blest?* while attempting to comprehend the contradictions that define the African situation, marks the connecting centre between the analytical and constructive phases in his fictional creation. Armah's earlier two novels, *The Beautyful Ones Are Not Yet Born* and *Fragments* attempted in different ways to capture the sense of betrayal and guilt that characterized the post-independent African situation. The protagonists in these two novels wage a lone battle for their cherished value-systems in a ramshackle society of fragmented vision. In his later novels, *Two Thousand Seasons* and *The Healers*, the total consciousness of a whole people is sought to be unfolded. In a constructive sweep of African history and ideals, Armah attempts to designate 'the way' of the people of a continent in the second phase.

Why Are We So Blest? marks the centre of the shift to a communal voice and the narrative of the novel explores, without explicitly moving away from the personal posture of the previous novels, the hard realities of the continent. It offers a fictional re-creation of the peculiar phenomenon of the exploited offering itself as an easy prey to the dehumanizing processes set in motion by colonialism proper which is a negation of hard-fought independence. The novel, as such, is an indictment of the self-destructive streak of a group ethic as much as an exposé of the destructive capabilities of the exploiters. Frantz Fanon while analysing the pitfalls of national consciousness prophesies that colonialist tendencies would be perpetuated in a different form in post-colonial Africa:

> History teaches us clearly that the battle against colonialism does not run straight away along the lines of nationalism. For a very long time the native devotes his energies to ending

> certain definite abuses: forced labour, corporal punishment, inequality of salaries, limitation of political rights, etc. This fight for democracy against the oppression of mankind will slowly leave the confusion of neo-liberal universalism to emerge, sometimes laboriously, as a claim to nationhood. It so happens that the unpreparedness of educated classes, the lack of practical links between them and the mass of the people, their laziness, and let it be said, their cowardice at the decisive moment of the struggle will give rise to tragic mishaps.[1]

In *Why Are We So Blest?*, the social and psychological factors which demarcate the distinction between the white and the black, the oppressor and the oppressed are portrayed in husband-mistress relationship. Modin's fatal attraction for his white mistress, Aimee, is presented in terms of Africa's contact with Europe which had left a debilitating impact on the native mind and which is at the back of their psyche.

The narrative of the novel is unfolded alternately, though not in a sequential order, from the point of view of Solo, Modin and Aimee, the three main protagonists of the novel. Intercepting the flow of these points of view are the diary entries of Modin and Aimee. Solo's narrative is punctuated with commentaries on the past, present and future of Africa, the different slices of which are connected by a sense of gloom. He is in possession of the diaries of Modin and Aimee which enable him to corroborate facts and view the life that has been lived against the background of his own failure in the revolutionary struggle. Although the purpose of Solo in re-arranging the pieces of their story together is self-admittedly 'littleness itself' it has wide-ranging implications in the context of personal and racial relations. The novel remains a complex study of contrasts in its thematic and structural dimensions and the fragmented narrative effectively captures all-pervading sense of failure.

Solo is a translator in the People's Union of Congheria, seat of the government in exile. He carries with him the twin failure of his own past and the burden of the African past. His participation in the revolutionary struggle leaves him with strong memories of failure and inadequacy on the one hand and desolation on the other. Although the details of his participation in the struggle and the reasons for his failure are not specified, we come to realize through the bits and pieces of his reminiscences that he opted out of the revolutionary struggle because of his reluctance 'to pretend.' It can safely be deduced from his realization that something went wrong not with Solo's participation but with the nature and orientation of the struggle itself. Solo sadly recalls how he had failed to develop 'the ability to do one thing, while saying and preferably also thinking another thing entirely' (14). Success, even in these circumstances depended on pretension and he preferred to remain a loser, 'life's failure,' when the 'successful livers are those with entrails hard enough to bear the contradiction and thrive on it' (14). The same corrupting and hypocritical influences that characterized the revolutionary struggle are perpetuated in post-independent African context and Solo considers himself a misfit in this sordid scheme of things. He stands apart from 'this ugliness, insistent and grim' (15) and his only preoccupation is 'with beautiful truths.' Like the man in *The Beautyful Ones Are Not Yet Born*, Solo refuses to compromise on basic values he cherishes most and is consequently faced with the prospect of being labelled a loser. He often wonders whether 'anything exists that is at the same time both beautiful and true' (15). He belongs to that category of people who want to bring 'what they do and what is done around them into the same territory as what they think and what they dream' (14).

The post-war scenario is presented in the predicament of the children who have been rendered fatherless. Solo watches orphans and beggars in the street and is engulfed by a sense of guilt. Having taken part in the revolutionary struggle in which a million people had sacrificed their lives, he feels 'he were responsible for their having been reduced to this state.' Death-inured children could now speak about the death of their fathers in a matter-of-fact manner. He wonders how they could have 'understood death and learned to live with it as part of life' (16). The questions of the one-legged man whom Solo meets in the hospital—'Who gained? Who won?'—underline the reasons for the failure of the struggle. The questions prompt Solo to draw a diagram of a vehicle moving upwards. The truck represents society while the fuel it consumes to move forward is like the sacrifice of the militants. He explains that the fuel, in the process of providing energy to the vehicle, has consumed itself suggesting that the persons who fought for independence gained nothing.

The post-revolutionary disillusionment is tellingly brought out in the running of People's Union of Congheria itself. Jorge Manuel and Estban Ngulo run the office whom Solo initially treats as 'brothers co-operating in the long fight.' But he soon perceives the division that exists between the two. Ngulo will remain a clerk while Jorge Manuel, the Foreign Minister of the government in exile would usurp 'the credit and sweetness' of their country's freedom. Solo prefers to call them 'man and his shadow.' Thus, he could only find 'inequalities within the struggle to end inequality.' The people are content with their masters' 'hypocritical honors' and the place itself is filled with 'peace indistinguishable from triviality.' The sense of failure introduced early in the novel is sustained throughout which in turn leads to the motif of death and the physical enactment of death-crescendo in the last pages of the novel.

Modin Dofu, the central character in the novel, is highly educated, intelligent, and pursues his studies at Harvard. Like Baako in *Fragments*, his problem is twofold: He remains a loner in America and cannot identify himself with the alien culture. Modin's problem is confounded by his inability to communicate with his own people back at home. His education proves to be a hurdle in the process of identification with his people. The white scholars attempt to make him feel 'all special on account of being with them' (121). They call him 'unique' and 'unusually intelligent,' which in fact increases his sense of alienation. He sees through their words and actions but still remains in America refusing to open himself out. When Oppenhardt is all praise for his academic record and his bright future in America, he asks himself: "Why see through Oppenhardt and let Harvard remain opaque to me?" The rejection of this 'manifest destruction' should have taken place early in his academic career in America for in due course the nagging question of identity makes him in effect a double exile. He is unable to translate his ideology into action nor can he remain attached to the place where he is best known by his colour and race and not through his individuality.

The sense of alienation forces Modin to seek companionship in sexual encounters with white women. Naita, his black girl-friend in America, warns against such misadventures in the initial stages itself. "There's nothing like friendship possible between us and them. You get involved with them, you're just dumb, that's all. They'll mess you up" (123). Modin later realizes that the words of Naita have literally come true with frightening consequences. He comes into contact with Mrs. Jefferson, the wife of one of his tutors in America, who shows unusual interest in Modin by virtue of his being black and as a result of her dissatisfaction with her ageing husband. Mrs. Jefferson's obsessive longing for Modin is not resisted by him. Inevitably the relationship gets exposed and Mr. Jefferson assaults him with a dagger. With multiple wounds, Modin finds himself in a hospital. In retrospect, he thinks that his life would not have been the 'blind drift' if he had asked himself 'real questions' and reached necessary answers. He is back to where he started, alone:

> Nothing surprising in all this. My life here has had a self-destructive swing all the time, only I haven't thought seriously about it. Loneliness. The search for a way out. Involvement. the thing you warned me against, Naita. Catastrophic involvement. Disaster. Exhaustion. Then withdrawal, intense, complete. Loneliness again. (156)

Even the realization of death-dealing psychological corruption does not prevent Modin from his subsequent association with Aimee Reitch. She is portrayed in the novel both as an individual and as a representative of her race, colour and continent. Aimee's interest in Modin is, like her revolutionary fervour, part of her search for new sensations. This is what, in fact, guided her to undertake a visit to an East African country where she had slept with the leaders of Moa-Moa rising and subsequently with the President of the Nationalist government. The episode is significant in that it portrays the depravity of the post-colonial political structures and also the morbid search of the Europeans for the exotic in black Africa. The first meeting of Modin with Aimee is in itself indicative of the things in store for him. They meet in a psychology laboratory where thresholds of pain are measured on a pain recorder. Most of the visitors, including Modin, record a normal of seven to eight points. Aimee, who came there for the sheer experience of it, records a high of thirteen points much to the surprise of all. Outside the laboratory, Aimee shows more than normal interest in Modin and he offers himself as an easy prey. Looking for a way out of his loneliness, Modin remains a spectator to the events that overpower him and from then on it was Aimee's voice that prevails all the way. The alienation of the individual, thus, is diligently portrayed as part of cultural hegemonism sought to be established by the white masters. This is evident in the character of Aimee. Her instinctual in-built mechanism not only saves her from being totally attached to her friend but enables her, in addition, to establish psychological superiority over her companion. The dividing agencies of cultural dichotomy and racial hiatus are so strong in this association that Modin remains a mute witness to and a helpless victim of the forces unleashed by his friendship with Aimee and gets carried away by his self-consuming streak.

II

Armah reposes immense faith in the artist-figure as a repository of light and wisdom in the midst of chaos and darkness. Like the man in *The Beautyful Ones Are Not Yet Born* and Naana and Baako in *Fragments*, Solo is a visionary. It was he who predicted the futility and fatality of the energy of Modin and Aimee which effectively exposes the helplessness of Solo on the one hand and the inaction that has become a hallmark of his life particularly after his disillusionment with the revolutionary struggle to bring in a new era. Solo often identifies with Modin. In the first instance, they had similar experiences in personal and then on the revolutionary front: 'I read him, watching me, a specter from an unwanted destiny, wondering how little time he had to go before his fire also went out and he too was reduced to me' (138). He is reminded of his own relationship with Sylvia, a white woman, which was broken off for racial reasons. The speed with which Modin's destruction materializes confirms the doubts and fears of Solo about the dangers involved in the relationship with the whites. In this context, it is also significant to note what he thinks about Aimee. He considers her an object, 'powerfully hurled against him from the barrel of a powerful, destructive culture' (115). It is evident that for him, she is more of a manifestation of the greed of her race and culture than an individual in flesh and blood. It is for these reasons that Solo feels guilty for not finding the means of Modin's escape. This is similar to the sense of guilt that overwhelms him for the failure of the struggle. In both the instances, he remained a mute witness to the process of disintegration.

Modin's problem must be viewed in terms of the isolation he experiences both for sociological and psychological reasons. In America, he is perceived only as a 'factor' and not as a fellow human being. The 'factor' was a black slave trader who acted as a middle-man in selling the slaves. His modern successors, the educated elite, who govern Africa are taken for granted by the whites and act accordingly. Modin confronts the contradiction of this situation when he is engaged in a discussion with Mike, a fellow scholar at Harvard. Mike reads out to him a write-up on America's blessedness published in the *Times* which is entitled 'Why Are Wo So Blest?' It clearly demarcates the distinction between the privileged and the unprivileged:

> The myth of paradise finds its full meaning here, in the new world—The blest among the blest know what this vision from the new world is. They see its oneness with whatever has been pure in the western traditions: the perfect symmetry of the Olympic ideal, the unsullied wholeness of that Christian Eden ignorant of the fall from Grace! (98-99)

Modin says that anyone who boasts about the settlers and ignores the mass-murder of the Indians is 'a street corner hustler, nothing more.' He further continues that Mike's forefathers wiped them out symbolically. Modin is only too aware of the other side of the 'genius' and 'blessedness' of the Europeans and aptly observes: "What the European riff-raff—your great ancestors—brought with them was the European genius for destroying everything—in an exaggerated form" (100). While Modin could counter the narcissistic arguments of the anonymous writer of the *Times* and the patronising attitude of Mike, he proves to be no match for the aggressive drive of Aimee and her domineering personality. She launches an uninhibited and multi-pronged assault on his personality fully exploiting his psychological disadvantages without any qualms. She is portrayed as being true to herself in selecting a prey, exploiting it to the last drop and finally letting destruction overpower her victim.

In her first sexual encounter with Modin, Aimee finds him no different from others, but she gradually converts him into an instrument to shake off her frigidity and become her own normal self. Once she realizes that he could be an effective weapon in regaining her womanliness, she does not want to lose him and becomes all the more overbearing. In bed with him, she imagines herself a memsahib whose husband, a repressive colonial administrator, comes home to find her making love with a houseboy. By fantasizing like this, she arouses herself and finds sexual satisfaction.

It is the superior agency that is set to win, by a complex set of psychological, sociological and cultural advantages, in a racial divide that manifests itself in personal relationships. Having committed itself to the process of continuing relationship the subjugated personality must always be on its guard or liberate itself from the corrupting influence and the dehumanizing death-dealing of the other. By all accounts, Modin is guilty of not resorting to either of the options. Solo, for instance, thinks that something could have been done by Modin to avoid the imminent:

> I read her: a devouring spirit, more than egotistic; her needs blast a path through everything around her. The world she inhabits is bent around herself. . . . His gentleness should not have gone to feed her hardness. (116)

The truth is that Modin could see that—her masochism, the cultural divide and his own tragedy. He could as well see through their words and deeds. What Solo thinks about Modin is complementary to what Modin thinks about himself:

> These things I was doing freely out of my own desire—they are also part of the larger scheme that aims at our destruc-

> tion. My friendships here have been different invitations to different kinds of death, calls to a spiritual disintegration far beyond the merely social disintegration. Africa has suffered since how many centuries? (158-59)

Modin's self-admitted spiritual disintegration in opting for a different kind of invitation to a different kind of death is indeed quite appalling. In fact, the moment he lands in the office of People's Union of Congheria along with Aimee in search of revolutionary 'action,' he seems to have accepted the inevitability of his disintegration and from then on it was a question of time and place for the inevitable to happen. In this self-consuming adventure of orgy and violence, Aimee has been the leader while Modin remains a mute follower. She shows him the way to death and destruction, preserving herself for hotter pursuits.

Aimee in her desire to take part in the revolutionary struggle, whatever the scene of it, is primarily motivated by her sadistic streak. She is guided by her intoxicating desire to find new sensations in different kinds of experiences, the same thing that has guided her to the psychology laboratory. Revolutionary action for her is an adventurous sport, exciting if seen first hand and stimulating if taken part in the game. This sadistic streak leads one to conclude that her sympathy for the liberation movement is only a self-made facade for her volatile sexual urges.

The persons-in-charge of the People's Union of Congheria try to dissuade and actually prevent them from joining the scene of struggle. They tell the couple that 'battle-field' is not a place for 'intellectuals' (252) and that they would be 'out of place' there. They firmly conclude that they would not enroll them into the ranks of the UPC but do not tell the truth on their face. In order to reassure them, they take an application from each of them and ask the couple to wait for the outcome. Solo, who was a witness to the discussion that ensues between Jorge Manuel and Estban Ngulo, knows that the couple would be kept waiting for decision indefinitely to the point of desperation. They seem to have made a fairly good assessment of the intentions of the pair, particularly of Modin which comes out in the words of Ngulo: "He is one of the intellectuals who wants to die. He should have the courage to do it himself. He can't come to us looking for an instrument of death" (255). The reply of Solo provides an instant comment on the devouring spirit of Aimee: "I don't think he needs an instrument of death, as you call it. . . . He may have found one. In which case what he needs is help" (255).

Even after repeated attempts they fail to get permission from the office of the UPC but still they persist with frequent visits to the office. Solo, who is in the know of things, offers them shelter in his house when they run out of money. Irrespective of Modin's wishes, Aimee flatly refuses his offer, preferring to stay in the filthy hotel which she terms as 'revolutionary.' In her perception, filth is synonymous with revolution. What she wants is a feel of it—a drenching and thorough experience of filth and revolution. Solo's first impression of the couple gets confirmed by Modin's helplessness and Aimee's sadistic streak. While reading the diaries, he himself is haunted by an eerie sense of insecurity:

> I search her book. What I find worsens my chagrin. It makes no sense. So much destructiveness caught in everything she said, everything she did, the way she moved, the tenor of her being. Why did he let her destroy him? I have said love, but that is an answer for fools. (149)

Their patience sufficiently tested, they undertake a journey of the desert which was under the control of the French Army. Modin, as on the previous occasions, finds himself an unwilling partner in the death-bound journey. But this time the decision—or the lack of it—proves fatal for him. The journey itself, with an aura of death and destruction looming large, creates a chilling effect while the actual death scene, in the last pages of the novel, turns out to be one of the most horrific in modern literature. It is the culmination of Aimee's aggressive experimentation with sexual encounters and Modin's deep-rooted psychological subjugation. All along the journey, Modin is nagged by the doubt that he is treading on a dangerous path, but when he gives vent to his feelings, he is snubbed by Aimee for being "bourgeoisie" in his thoughts. They pursue their journey in the desert aimlessly until they meet the Army Personnel in a jeep who are on patrol. The colour disparity of the couple accentuates their sadistic tendencies and their actions cross the limits of barbarism. They undress Modin, humiliate him, arouse him, cut his male organ and leave him in the desert to die. Aimee does not feel the pinch of his suffering, but is engrossed in her own lustful thoughts at not having made a final contact with the already dazed, bleeding Modin. He is, thus, turned into an object, a plaything to gratify the sense of a bulldozing superiority on the one hand and insatiable lust on the other which however, find a similar wave-length in sadism. The white Army Personnel leave Aimee near Laccryville.

III

Modin in his thoughts and in his action seems to be two different persons altogether. In his thoughts, he gives the impression of a genius at work, which is really what he is—an African 'rarity.' He considers his own life as an off-shot of collective predicament. He ardently believes in the Maji, the workable system, that 'special something Africans needed to neutralize the material destructiveness of Europe' since he realizes that the 'revolutionary ideal is an actual, working egalitarian society' (222).

The observations Modin makes in his thesis are important not merely at a purely theoretical level, but provide a sharp contrast to Modin's energy-in-flux. The main postulate of his thesis is that the search for a workable system is a continuous process—an educational and a warring process—'for creating new anti-European, anti-imperial, anti-elitist values' (222). The 'non-elitist methods of disseminating consciousness' not only involve destruction of elite structures, 'the rites of secrecy, mystification,' but paves the way for a positive direction, the Maquis. It quite naturally follows that Modin should question himself, his own standing on the elite structures which are like 'thick walls.' The thick walls, the elaborate rituals of education, Modin thinks, create proud tools, thus preventing them from taking part in the ongoing destruction. The inevitable conclusion he arrives at is an echo of the feelings of the oppressed: 'This system has no justification' (224). As a result, he is no longer interested in the pursuit of 'academic nonsense' which has effectively created barriers between him and his own people. It is evident that Modin's commitment to his people, unlike Aimee's pretensions, is genuine.

Modin's views on communal well-being which he terms as the maquis, at the societal level, and on his own inadequacy to partake in that process, his isolation and death-bound journey are quite accurate in that they provide a fairly objective self-assessment. But the moment he sees Aimee he gets hypnotically anaesthetized and falters—at the cost of his individuality and ultimately his life. This contradiction between self-professed and firmly-held views and instinctual drives is not a peculiar phenomenon in the African context, given the peculiar attributes of colonial hangover operating at every conceivable sphere of experience. In dealing with the phenomenon of the 'been-to' in Armah's second novel, it has been demonstrated earlier that Baako, in spite of or because of clear vision, goes mad, unable to cope with the conflicting values caught as he is between the two worlds of personal integrity and the societal demands the miniature representation of which is the family.

Modin's relationship with Aimee must be viewed in terms of Fanon's exposition of colonial experience in psychological terms. According to Fanon, the biological aspect is the immediate and inescapable element which the racialist ideology uses as its starting-point of exploitation. Among the multitude of cliches mobilised against the Negro the sexual aspect takes on a special significance. Fanon says: 'It is in his corporeality that the Negro is attacked. It is as a concrete personality that he is lynched.'[3] One attributes to the Negro an abnormal sexual potency bordering on the perverse. Fanon corroborates his thesis by his own experiences as a practising psychiatrist: in all cases of Negrophobia the patients' sex life was found to be abnormal. The psychological and sociological factors which initiate the process of Modin's destruction are clearly exposed by his contact with Aimee.

The psychological implications of the brutal way in which Modin was murdered by the white army personnel could also be found in Fanon's postulates. He explains that the hatred of the whites against the Negroes stems from a feeling of sexual inferiority. Consequently, the lynching of a Negro would have to be interpreted as sexual revenge. Fanon, in fact, interprets racism as the protection of the civilized white man's irrational longing for the lost paradise of sexual license onto the Negro: 'Projecting his own desires onto the Negro, the white man behaves "as if" the Negro really had them.'[4] Viewed in this light, Armah's *Why Are We So Blest*? becomes a fictional representation of Fanon's stratagem in approaching colonial/neo-colonial structures.

Solo, in moments of retrospection, appears more like a commentator on colonial experience and its microcosmic representation in the life of Modin. He is often invaded by pangs of guilt for not having taken the initiative to avert Modin's tragedy. The nagging suspicion that he himself remained helpless in not being able to stop Modin's destruction underlines his point of view throughout the narrative: 'Whatever I tell myself, I cannot escape the chagrin of not being able to stop his destruction' (115). But in reality he could have helped little. Modin's energy was not coursing through a life-generating path as he had intended to but was inexorably caught 'in too small a space, born for destruction' (137).

Modin's problems and experiences in America must be viewed in the light of the previously enacted drama of cultural confrontation of the black psyche in a white landscape. Modin is considered unusually intelligent, a rarity, but a 'rarity to keep the blest entertained,' a black who is only a 'factor' in the white scheme of things. Modin, in spite of his intelligence, remains an anonymous black and he had to shed his identity and merge with the general phenomenon of the 'factor' to entertain the blessed ones. The treatment meted out to him being the same in every case, proper nouns are turned into attributives.

In such a suffocating atmosphere, the individual is driven to be on guard against an overdose of retribution and patronizing scorn for being an African, the cumulative fall-out of which is further alienation and psychological distance from the surroundings. The seeming helplessness of the individual forces Modin to take recourse to certain thoughts and actions that vitiate his psychic equilibrium. Constantly haunted by a sense of insecurity and loneliness, Modin asserts himself in sexual encounters with white women. He warns himself against such misadventures, but remains helpless. Once the contact is established with Aimee, he finds little means of escape. Their relationship is not based on reciprocity. The devouring spirit of Aimee takes in whatever Modin could muster and offers only her greed in return. The psychological explanation of the complex racial relations carries with it an element of imminence.

The colonized man is handicapped in establishing contacts with his environment through his complexes and feelings of insecurity. Eventually he becomes, in Fanon's phrase the 'prisoner of an unbearable insularity.' Fanon observes: 'In the man of colour there is a constant effort to run away from his own individuality, to annihilate his own presence. Whenever a man of colour protests, there is alienation.'[5] Conversely, any attempt on his part to find a way out of the solitude inevitably lands him in the white world. Interracial sexual contacts in particular seem to afford the colonized a solution to his problems, albeit only in the private world. In actual fact such problems being the product of objective conditions, do not allow of any subjective solution. The man of colour, Fanon observes, by having a sexual relationship with a white woman takes revenge on the colonial master and at the same time proves that he is his equal, a member of the human race.[6]

Solo's life and attitude is complementary to Modin. Solo also gets involved with a white woman, Sylvia, but the relationship does not play havoc in his personal life since it was aborted even before take-off. Solo's sense of failure is borne out of his disillusionment with the struggle. Modin manifests the inevitability of what Solo would have got had he continued his relationship with Sylvia. For this reason, the failure of Solo compared to Modin's, appears to be modest and carries with it a modicum of respectability.

Armah's fragmented narrative is truly attested by the sense of suffering caused by the shattering impact of colonialism. Moving back and forth in time and space, it effectively captures the vicissitudes of the post-colonial African context. In this attempt to capture contemporaneity in freeze-shots and close-ups and in its drive to define the nature and extent of the devastating impact of colonialism in the personal world in which all things are blown apart, the novel remains an integral part of Armah's fictional strategy in approaching the African reality. By implication, it also suggests a meaningful direction to the ongoing struggle in the process of decolonizing the African mind.

Why Are We So Blest? marks the end of the analytical phase in Armah's literary career and sets the tone and context for the brilliant exposition of the group consciousness in the constructive phase as evidenced in the last two novels. Solo, the artist-figure, paves the way for seers, prophets, utterers and healers, the exponents of positive direction, the Maquis of Modin's vision and the course of which is defined by Solo: 'In this wreckage there is no creative art outside the destruction of the destroyers. In my people's world, revolution would be the only art, revolutionaries the only creators. All else is part of Africa's destruction' (231). The statement not only opens up possibilities for a literary warfare against colonialism of all shades but defines the fictional oeuvre of Armah as well.

NOTES

1. Ayi Kwei Armah, *Why Are We So Blest?* (New York: Doubleday, 1972; London: Heinemann Educational Books, 1974; Nairobi: East African Publishing House, 1974). All page references are to the Heinemann edition.
2. Frantz Fanon, *The Wretched of the Earth* (London: Penguin Books, 1967), p. 119.
3. Frantz Fanon, *Black Skin, White Masks* (London: MacGibbon and Kee, 1968), p. 163.
4. *Ibid.*, p. 165.
5. *Ibid.*, p. 60.
6. *Ibid.*, p. 81.

Destruction of Destroyers:
Two Thousand Seasons

Two Thousand Seasons,[1] in its sweep and presentation, defies classifications in the sense that as a piece of fiction, it can also be considered as a study in history, anthropology, and aesthetic dialectics. Its encapsulating view informs and derives its strength from rhythmic patterns and structural polarities. It provides a perfect instance of the context informing the interaction between the content and form, ideology and action. Because of its wide range, depth and profound human concerns, the novel becomes an epic in its presentation, mytho-poetic in its texture, historical in perspective and continental in bearings.

The novel's macro-microcosmic vision is presented in dialectical terms and in the articulation of corroboratives and alternatives. It is a literary manifesto for the collective credo of a race and a continent. In its dialectical sweep, it is a bombshell directed against the exploiters for the liberation of both mind and body. It is a war-cry against colonialism of all hues and shapes from a literary standpoint. The novel's collective voice in the form of 'we,' with its shared suffering and group ethic, is reinforced by the author's inspirational and socialistic affirmation. Besides, the underlying moral vision directs and decides the behavioural patterns of good and evil, beauty and ugliness and integrity and disintegration. Thus, the novel is many things at a time and it opens the floodgates of new ventures and exciting possibilities. In the process, it transcends the realm of its existence and elevates the range of experience of the reader.

The critical opinion on the novel is diverse and contradictory. Bernth Lindfors represents the colonialist school of thought and dismisses the novel in terms of "a philosophy of paranoia, an anti-racist racism—in short, negritude reborn. In place of a usable historical myth, *Two Thousand Seasons* overschematizes the past, creating the dangerous kind of lie that Frantz Fanon used to call a 'mystification.'[2] Kirsten Holst Peterson expresses her unhappiness with the novel when she says: "No one could object to a search for 'connectedness' as opposed to 'fractured vision' or an affirmation of the female principle, but when everything is seen in the light of black, good/white, evil dichotomy one wonders what is the purpose of it. A reaffirmation of racism?" It is ironical that Peterson should borrow Cesaire's words and try 'to restore the perspective' decrying 'racism': "No race has a monopoly of beauty, intelligence, strength and there is room for all in the rendezvous of conquest."[3]

Emmanuel Ngara, on the other hand, holds that *Two Thousand Seasons* is a great epic. He says: "The amount of material covered and the vision given to the African people are fantastic and admirable. There is nothing so far written in African fiction to surpass its excellence of language, its epic splendour, its immense moral earnestness."[4] According to Hugh Webb,

> The work proceeds from a very clear awareness that culture is not neutral politically (to use Meredith Tax's phrase) and that it is impossible for it to be so. Such an awareness carried with it the realization that men and women can fully comprehend their own existence only when it is seen as something historically conditioned. Armah, by portraying changes of viewpoint and relationships, changes of possible and actual resolutions (as forms of literary organization) attempts a cultural synthesis of the highest order.[5]

Isidore Okpewho interprets the novel in mytho-poetic terms. He says that the younger generation of novelists are

> guided by a certain revolutionary conscience and do not think the old mythology provides sufficient answers for the problems of contemporary African society. In their works we find an intensification of the critical spirit, an urge to overhaul the foundations on which the old social outlook was erected, and consequently an energy directed at creating a new mythology that would offer for the projected or emergent society a firmer road to self-realization than could be

> found in the older traditions. We may therefore wish to call the tendency here revealed *tradition* revised. Perhaps no recent work better demonstrates this urge to review the old mythic tradition and furnish new hopes than Armah's *Two Thousand Seasons.*[6]

Rand Bishop says that the novel represents "an exciting new development that sets apart from the rest of his contemporaries." He prophesies that it will take sometime for the novel to establish itself: "The impact of the novel . . . will be immense, once its form is fully appreciated and its message is widely disseminated."[7]

Two Thousand Seasons aims at decolonizing the mind of the oppressed providing an impetus to the liberating forces initiated in the previous novels. Seen from this perspective, the earlier novels become a call for social reform rather than a distorted version of the society. The shift from individual to communal axis is not a sudden or accidental development in *Two Thousand Seasons*. In *The Beautyful Ones Are Not Yet Born*, the man, within his limitations, wages a grim battle against a corrupt social order and moral depravity. The complexion of the situation gets transformed with his wife finally attesting to his integrity at the end. It is the ultimate reward for him since he is a lone individual whereas the family is a miniature representation of the society with its myriad demands. In *Fragments*, individualism is not offered as an answer or an alternative to a corrupt community. Baako's nervous breakdown is an ironic comment on the pitfalls of individualism also. In *Two Thousand Seasons*, Armah invariably returns to the issue of the retrieval of the individual mind and also the community as part of a grand scheme.

One cannot miss the overwhelming influence of Fanon on Armah as evidenced in *Two Thousand Seasons.* The novel bears the stamp of *The Wretched of the Earth* in terms of the principle of violence. It also reinforces Modin's belief in *Why Are We So Blest?* Modin asserts that the war against the invaders should be an educational process for creating 'new anti-European, anti-elitist values.' The epic-dialectic form of the novel is aimed towards what Soyinka and Dennis Brutus have called for in their Declaration of African Writers (1975) 'the full retrieval of the African past in the quest for a contemporary self-apprehension and design for the future.' This is consistent with Armah's thought-process as discernible in his essay 'African Socialism: Utopian or Scientific?' in which he defines community in terms of 'shared sufferings and shared hopes.' As a result, the intensity of suffering is alleviated, since it is shared collectively on behalf of the community. Thus, the issues of socialism, Pan-Africanism and national realities are important in Armah's work. The interaction between the local and national realities must pave way for a pragmatic socialist ideal. Armah realizes the dialectics of the processes involved in this connection. According to Armah,

> the socialist tradition itself is a mytho-poetic system. The greater source of power and influence available to the socialist tradition is its acceptance and imaginative use of the archetypal dream of total liberation . . . the thoroughgoing negation of repressive facts of real life.[8]

This process is particularly pronounced in *Two Thousand Seasons.* The novel is marked by structural parallelism as evidenced in the first part covering a mass of humanity and the second part limited to a core group of militant-liberators.

II

The first person plural 'we' is the operative word in the novel. It decides the voice of the community and also the structure of the novel. Its functional significance gains momentum as it informs the credo of a mass of people and also expresses itself through the liberating process initiated by a select group. In the process, it makes the narrative move into the traditional realm of the oral narrative. The voice of the speaker which includes the authorial voice is the moral index, with his communal audience sharing the group experience. Besides integrating the action of the novel, it also helps to thread the various images and motifs which recur in the novel with consistent regularity. The use of the plural voice helps Armah in the process of reassessment of centuries of experience by means of a viable native standpoint:

> Trapped now in our smallest self, we, repositories of the re-

> membrance of the way violated, we, portion that sought the meaning of Anoa's utterance in full and found another home on this same land, we, fraction that crossed mountains, journeyed through forests, shook off destruction only to meet worse destruction, we, people of the fertile time before these schisms, we, life's people, people of the way, trapped now in our smallest self, that is our vocation: to find our larger, our healing self, we, the black people. (9)

For the purpose of reconstruction, Armah feels the need to break the colonial myths about the Africans and their societies. It is all the more imperative when the natives are pitted against the combined might of the European and Arab destroyers with their record of centuries of exploitation. Armah thrusts upon himself, in right earnest, the task of setting the record straight:

> We are not a people of yesterday. Do they ask how many single seasons we have flowed from our beginnings till now? We shall point them to the proper beginning of their counting. (1)

The collective voice of 'we,' serves yet another important purpose. It helps Armah to place the action of the novel outside the frame of the Western concept of time. Armah presents each year in terms of two seasons—dry and wet: 'But why should we make an unending remembrance of drought and rain, the mere passage of seasons?' (6) It provides an occasion for Armah to study critically the history of one thousand years of Africa.

The collective voice of 'we,' thus determining its own time-frame, projects a larger perspective in respect of colonial holocaust and its ramifications. As the collective predicament is subjected to scrutiny, it is made clear that in spite of the wide-ranging destruction sought to be perpetuated against the way of the people, the colonial experience is only a temporary phenomenon out of which they are capable of emerging out with a clearer vision. The recapitulation of two thousand seasons, or one millennium, helps to unravel the different phases of the confrontation.

In this broad time-frame, the mythical voice of Anoa integrates and reinforces the action of the novel linking all the generations of two thousand seasons. According to the legend, Anoa, even as a young girl, was invested with visions of future which she attempted to share with her people. Anoa's utterance is marked by an uncanny sense of foreboding about the future predicament of a whole people:

> Two thousand seasons: a thousand you will spend descending into abysses that would stop your heart and break your mind merely to contemplate. Two thousand seasons: a thousand dry, a thousand moist. (16)

The associative portrayal of 'the way' delineates the course of action which the plural voice of 'we' and Anoa's utterance have set before the community as its goal. The need of the moment is to recapture 'the way' of the people which they had lost for reasons both internal and external. 'The way' defines the mental attitude of a collective psyche and the culture of a community besides showing the way for the future. It is the path of virtue, of integral vision and wholeness. The novelist seeks to emphasize the concept in terms of alternatives and irreconcilable polarities.

The way of the oppressors is the path of crime and violence. They plant nothing. Their harvest is 'rape' and exploitation. The way of the people, on the other hand, is generosity and fertility. The way is opposed to fragmentation. Creation and connectedness are the two important facets of the way:

> Our vocation goes against all unconnectedness. It is a call to create the way again, and where even the foundations have been assaulted and destroyed, where restoration has been made impossible, simply to create the way. (8)

The road of the white destroyers is the antithesis of the way of the people.

> The destroyers take. That is their way. They know nothing of reciprocity. The road to death—that is their road. (7)

Thus, the group concept as symbolized in the collective voice of 'we' with its self-determined time-frame, Anoa's utterance, and the way of the people determine the basic structure and tenor of the novel.

III

Armah launches an offensive while parading the predators, the destroyers, the askari zombis and the oppressors. The natives are aware of the fact that the land originally belongs to them. They know that they are one people. They are not static people hating motion and change. The destroyers distort this truth:

> We are not a stagnant people, hating motion. . . . That we the black people are one people we know destroyers will travel long distances in their minds and out to deny you this truth. We do not argue with them, the fools. (3)

They had a long tradition of culture which enabled them to develop a set of their own beliefs, thoughts, and 'many wonderings' in tune with the native soil. But the advent of the white predators from the desert, the Arabs, and the white destroyers from the sea, the European colonizers, put the native institutions to a remorseless destruction.

The prophetic voice of Anoa warned that the generosity of the people would be their undoing. The voice urged them to move away from the path of generosity and return to reciprocity. One thousand seasons of scattering and another thousand seasons of groping has much to do with their 'tragic flaw' of giving without any thought of returns. The predators and destroyers exploited this weakness of the people to the full extent. The imminent foreboding of doom is marked by self-examination. The present degradation is the result of the people's 'blinding abundance' and the consequent loss of 'the way' which is the way of reciprocity:

> Reciprocity, that is the way you have forgotten, the giving, the receiving, the living alternation of the way. The offerers, those givers who do not receive, they are mere victims. That is what in the heedless generosity of your blinding abundance you have turned yourselves into. (17)

The authorial voice corroborates with the voice of Anoa. In the Prologue, the author sets in motion the dynamics of reciprocity. The images employed in this connection are spring water and desert. It is the natural function of the spring to flow and give in abundance, while the desert takes and absorbs everything, giving nothing. The desert keeps expanding whereas the spring runs the risk of going dry if it attempts to change the desert. The natives should never look upto the Europeans for guidance in the same way as the desert is not the direction of the spring flow since the 'desert blasts with destruction whatever touches it.'

The structural polarities involved in the novel are also indicated in the Prologue. As the strategy is to open up possibilities for lost hope the juxtaposition of the macro-microcosms is intended to realize the ultimate 'way' of the people. Anoa's prophecy of 'a thousand seasons wasted wandering amazed along alien roads, another thousand spent finding paths to the living way' provides a basis for action and the structural strategy of the novel.

IV

The plural voice of 'we' in the first four chapters invokes a shared tale and a communal experience, ranging from the rule of women—'the time of fertility' to the patriarchal society. This part also covers the voice of many generations in exile. They are driven away from their native lands by the predators from the desert. But in their new settlements, they confront another powerful enemy—'the destroyers from the sea.' The search for a home and the crisis of identity suggest the alienation of a whole community on its own soil.

The struggle against the whiteness of destruction and the sense of alienation are depicted in the second part comprising the last three chapters. The struggle for liberation is portrayed in terms of mental and physical regeneration. The use of violence, in the process, is real and symbolic at the same time. It is carried out by a small group of revolutionaries inspired by the healers. The healers' work of inspiration is psychological and hence, symbolic. The revolutionaries resort to rightful violence for the liberation from the all-pervading influence of the whiteness of destruction.

V

The first part of the novel in a macrocosmic vision encompasses Anoa's warning about the loss of the 'way,' the long epic journey of the people in search of a 'new home' and also the betrayal by the 'ostentatious cripples' who were hand in glove with the white destroyers. The unifying principle of fertility is introduced straightaway in the novel. The male domination in a patriarchal society is marked by greed, jealousy and laziness. Their contempt for justice resulted in internecine struggles and a 'festival of annihilation.' They smashed up everything. It was left for the women to begin the work of creation from the scratch. The 'masculine carnage' thus gave way to a healing process.

There was an abundance of provisions during the women's rule, since it was creation's time. The new order deprived the men of all unearned privileges and ordained that all enjoyment must flow from the outcome of 'work accomplished.' But this phase also gave birth to generosity. They did not worry about receiving as they were accustomed to producing without any thought of returns. The general astonishment at the onslaught of the white destroyers was, therefore, sudden and shattering.

The predators, in fact, came like beggars. The natives pitied them with their look of hunger in body and soul. It was part of the way to provide sustenance to the needy. But their abundance proved to be 'a giddy disequilibrium' swallowing 'all lasting balance' (18). The beggars who came like guests grew stronger and in the fullness of their strength they turned into predators against 'an easy host' (19). Thirty days of violence and massacre made them masters over their hosts.

The predators turned the native women into playthings in their sexual orgies. The physical and moral degradation of the Arab predators is depicted in the scenes of sexual orgies and their possessive manic state. Hussein, the twin brother of Hassan the Syphilitic, Faisal and Mohammed are all caught in the quagmire of their own degeneration and perversion. The women who were mere instruments of their perverted happiness and sexual orgies hand them over the reward they deseve—violent and suffocating death.

The early attack by the Arab marauders from the desert produced a debilitating effect on the minds of the natives and turned them into willing slaves who later came to be known as askari zombis. These slaves were used as mercenaries to liquidate the natives who were engaged in offering resistance to the marauders' destructive work. They, thus, did the 'blood work' of the predators. The mindless were truly experts in their violent job of killing all those caught trying to end the oppression. The predators reduced them into stooges and beasts for an easy manipulation—'beasts they could command, things they could manipulate' (29). Following the death of the predators at the hands of the native women, they went on a killing spree without paying heed to Nandi's wise counsel. Nandi's question and her exhortation—

> That should have been your work: killing your people's destroyers. You did not do it, the work of your life. Instead you chose the work of walking corpses, killing your own people (25).

goes unheeded and she is killed by her own grandson. In such an eerie and gloomy situation, marked by senseless violence and ghastly murders, there can be no possibility of liberation, much less creation.

The roots of the 'long bafflement at the heavy phenomenon of the slave forever conditioned against himself' (26) could be found in the elevated slave-position of the askari-zombis. The people thought that they would change with time. They were too generous on this score. When the predators came a second time they found ready tools of murder in the askari zombis with their secret wishes of destruction against their own people.

In the aftermath of the women's revolt against the first destroyers, male domination came into being. Against the background of the women's rule, men occupied all positions of responsibility and power heralding a hereditary and hierarchical pattern of social living. The caretakers were always engaged in quarrels which were not related to the problems of the people. Classes and divisions came into existence and the schisms between the rulers and the ruled, the people and their chosen representatives became wider.

The second onslaught of the predators was more cunning than the first. This time they did not depend upon force alone. They used guile to exploit the divisions among the caretakers. They also employed their religion to capture the souls of the natives making them 'soulless things.' The new religion, in fact, is a fraud on the native people. It manifests in the form of cheating and violence:

> With their surroundings they know but one manner of relationship, the use of violence. Against other peoples they recommend to each other the practice of robbery, cheating, at best a smiling dishonesty. Among them the sphere of respect is so shrunken they themselves have become sharp-clawed desert beasts, preying against all. (40)

The natives could not accept a road of life 'constructed by a god of hate' (42). There was no hesitation among the different clans with regard to the course of action open to them. They begin their long journey in search of a new home leaving everything behind and 'seeking unknown places' where their spirits would 'still have room to move.' (42)

The search for a new home is marked by a sense of exile, hope, promise and adventure. The mass movement of a whole people assumes epic proportions. They find, in the process of their long journey, a natural ally in the form of Nature itself. They cross mountains, land of hostile ones, and the 'land of an unwonted fertility.' They develop friendship with people who were already settled there, but continue their journey through 'frightening forests, strange sly grass, slushing waters and a maddening abundance of encumbring vegetation' (49). They spent a hundred seasons in this painfully slow journey marked by the advent of new generations.

The epic march is ultimately rewarded. The pathfinders, Noliwe and Ningome, take them to a place where vegetation, water and animal life offer a unified picture of harmony. The presence of human life adds fullness to Nature. The people find the new place enchanting and beautiful. Even the seers find it difficult to describe it in apt terms:

> With what shall the utterers' tongue stricken with goodness, riven silent with the quiet force of beauty, with which mention shall the tongue of the utterers begin a song of praise whose perfect singers have yet to come? (56)

The new home is named after the great prophetess and utterer, Anoa, herself. The land is beautiful and 'should have been perfect for the way.' But it is a land 'that will yet be,' as the beautiful ones are yet to be born. The 'ostentatious cripples' emerged once again to destroy the cherished ideals of the seers of the way. They also paved the way for the ensuing threat from the sea, the advent of the white destroyers, the European colonizers.

Armah treats the caretakers and the local chiefs of the people with utter disdain. Instead of engaging themselves in the task of construction and re-creation in the process of finding the way of the people, they were interested in 'the external, the superficial and the manipulable' (63). Bentum, Korbo, Tutu and Koranche, all caretakers, impose themselves upon 'a people too weary of strife to think of halting them.' In the fullness of their dreams and greed, 'the spirit of community is raped by worshippers of impressive trash' (63). They were simply finding ways to turn the whole community into a lifeless thing—'their crutch.' It was during king Koranche's rule that the white destroyers came from the sea.

VI

The second part of the novel signifies the juxtaposition of the structural polarities in the novel. The plural voice of 'we' in this part personifies the sense of liberation and the revolutionary fervour of a militant group of young men and women—'eleven girls and nine boys.'

Although the section deals with 'another thousand seasons' spent in the search for the 'way,' the time-span and action covered in this section is, to a large extent, limited. The action takes place precisely during the regimes of king Koranche and prince Bentum. The shift from general to the particular is marked by a swift turn of emphasis which is appropriate to the theme of the novel. The long epic journey included in the first part requires a scrutiny of the movement of generations and the collective plight. The realization of the way of the people is depicted in the second part in the collective predicament of a select group which represents the credo of a mass of people.

The core group of young revolutionaries, before they launch a vigorous search for the lost way, become skilled in games and 'dances of childhood.' They also learn skills such as farming, rowing and fishing. In the process, they are guided, trained and inspired by fundis, experts in different fields of learning and practical experience. The attempts of the fundis are not confined to mere training of the young in various skills. They are oriented to finding the way. The fundis are pained by the distance between the way and their people, the way and the seats of power directed against their own people. They educate the young people that their skills would be meaningless if they are 'actually turned like a weapon against their own people.' The learning itself becomes a mere waste if it is not guided by an awareness of their predicament:

> The skills themselves were mere light shells, needing to be filled out with substance coming from our souls (86).

Isanusi is the most articulate of the fundis. People respect his words and even king Koranche is afraid of him. He warns Koranche against welcoming the white destroyers. The young revolutionaries, before they are initiated into action, also benefit from Isanusi's analytical prowess and historical knowledge. He embodies the wisdom of the traditional world and the revolutionary spirit of the modern age. While analysing the point of conflict between the European colonizers and the natives, he observes:

> These white men, they do not want to be a part of us. But here they have come claiming they have crossed the sea from wherever it is they come from just to do us good. They are pretenders. They are liars. We have asked them for nothing. We should not let them come among us. They have no desire to live with us. They will live against us (98).

King Koranche symbolizes the greed of native kings for the gifts of the white destroyers. He does not hesitate to betray and destroy his people in pursuit of his selfish ends. He uses arms against the people in a gory scene of violence and destruction. Even Isanusi, the healer and the spokesman of the people, is banished for not uttering the praises of the king and the white enslavers.

Isanusi who lives in the forest is a conscience-keeper of the natives. He also works as a catalyst in the process of reconstruction.

The work of the healer is not complete with mere awakening but includes creation as well. Isanusi lives in the fifth grove of the forest in the company of Idawa who proves to be a sustaining and an inspiring principle in his life. He waits for an opportune moment to strike at the roots of the evil they are up against and to begin the process of finding the way of the people.

The core group of young men and women are tricked into slavery by king Koranche who sells them to the white destroyers in exchange for some paltry gifts. The young men and women are subjected to the most inhuman treatment following their enslavement. They also become witness to and victims to gruesome acts of ugliness and violence by the white destroyers during their transit in a ship. Hundreds of slaves are hoarded together in a dingy compartment in the ship amid stench and rot. Those who fall victims to contagious diseases are mercilessly thrown into the sea. Enslavement binds them together and even as their numbers grow, the desire to free themselves grows intense. When the opportunity comes, they pick up enough courage to attack the white enslavers with vengeance and free themselves.

The core group becomes a militant revolutionary outfit fired by a desire to find the way, the way of the soil, of reciprocity and wholeness. They are guided and inspired by Isanusi. The core group mobilizes others into an organized force to realize their cherished goal. The militant group's close association with Isanusi is a practical demonstration of the fusion of revolutionary ideology with practice and of strategy with action.

He makes them realize that this is not a momentary sense of revenge inspired by rage. They are guided by an awareness that this is a life's work:

> This has been no useless explosion of rage animating us, hurling us singly into the brief, senseless acts of momentary, particular revenge. In us has been the need to spend life against the present killing arrangements, destruction's established system; to spend life cutting through deceiving superfices to reach again the essential truths the destroyers must hide from spirits if their white road is to prevail; to spend life acting on the truth against destruction's whiteness; to spend

> life working with our people, searching for paths to our way. (157-58)

In these surroundings 'blighted with death's tinsel,' the work of destruction's destruction is the work of 'undying worth.' This is no harried vision with 'the sweety anticipation of impatient profit.' They are clear in their vision and the goal they have set before themselves:

> This lifework, its fruit should be the birth of new seers, other hearers, more numerous utterers. And the fruit of all our lifework together: that should be destruction's destruction. (158)

Juma, who had once served the white destroyers before joining the group, comes forward to train the others in shooting. Having learnt the subtleties of the art, they plan to attack the 'stone place' at Poano, the symbol of white authority. Again, Isanusi guides the members of the revolutionary group by negotiating with Kamuzu who has a pathological hatred for the princes of Poano and their parasites. The decision to attack the palace of Poano is followed by careful planning and organization. Some members of this group gather the minutest details of the stone place. Kamuzu enacts the role of a mediator with the white enslavers on behalf of Isanusi posing as a chieftain. Kamuzu asks the white masters to give a large quantity of weapons in exchange for slaves. On the pretext of examining the guns, Isanusi and other members of the group enter the palace and launch an offensive. They seize the palace and send a message through prince Bentum to king Koranche that those whom he had destroyed still remembered him.

They take away large quantities of arms to increase the stores they 'had hidden along the safe half-circle from the cave to the fifth grove' (165). From this strategic place, they continue their offensive attacking seven ships, destroying the destroyers in them and freeing the captives.

Isanusi's doubts about Kamuzu prove prophetic as he becomes a replica of the chief of the white destroyers, the one they used to call the governor. In his greed, he starts negotiations with the white masters. The militant group mobilizes its strength and returns to forest, leaving Kamuzu behind to be hanged by the destroyers and the parasites.

Isanusi reminds the members of the group that all that they did would be fruitless if they forget 'the way' of the people's understanding. They launch their offensive against the ships carrying captives and liberate them. Of the five hundred liberated, thirty members—twenty four women and six men—join the ranks of the militant group and they return to their work, 'unending work against destruction' (177).

King Koranche had nightmares about Isanusi and on the advice of the white destroyers, he announces rewards for those who capture him. The militant group foils two such attempts at capturing Isanusi. Following the counsel of the white masters, king Koranche and his princes and parasites also begin to swell the number of their askaris. The destroyers also bring in a heavy load of arms in preparation for the imminent strife. Isanusi prepares to go to the place where they had secretly hidden their arms on a hill. In the process, he is betrayed by Fosu, one of the new entrants into the ranks of the group. Before his death Isanusi not only kills the betrayer and two other askaris, but also saves the lives of Jumo and Kisa by his peremptory shout. Thus, the healers' work of destruction's destruction and creation is brought out in Isanusi's death also.

The members of the militant outfit pick up the threads from Isanusi and carry their offensive straight into Koranche's palace. They destroy the askaris in the night and capture Koranche, Otumfer, the flatterer, and other parasites. At dawn, they are brought to the largest of the public places to the beat of the drums. Abena speaks eloquently about the betrayal by king Koranche and the destruction wrought out by such parasites. King Koranche confesses his guilt in public and Abena herself shoots him to death at the end of his tale.

VII

The climax of the novel is the culmination of the contrasting values, patterns and systems set on a course of imminent collision.

It achieves a synthesis of the highest order marking the unity and wholeness of the novel. The collective voice of the communal experience takes over in the last few pages of the novel and realizes that perfect senses provide an answer and a counterpoint to the selfish desires and fragmented vision of the destroyers. The way of the people recognises connectedness as a part of its integral vision:

> There is no beauty but in relationships. Nothing cut off by itself is beautiful. Never can things in destructive relationships be beautiful. All beauty is in the creative purpose of our relationships; all ugliness is in the destructive aims of the destroyers' arrangements (206).

The violence resorted to by the core group is on the Fanonist lines. Counter-violence is needed for a return to the beautiful path ahead. Creation of life and destruction of the destroyers as discernible in the novel are closely interlinked and become synonymous with constructive connection with the way. Armah espouses and justifies violence on the course of confrontation with alien marauders. Creation entails connectedness, the 'larger circle.' Connectedness, in its wake, calls for destruction's destruction. This, in turn, is the preparation for and the beginning of creation's work. And yet, the people do not utter the praise of arms. Their purpose is more profound.

The conclusion of the novel also presents the true concerns of Armah in a proper perspective. The colonial holocaust, though a dehumanizing experience, could be resisted and successfully fought against. Besides, the axis of the broad framework of past, present and future so effectively brought out so far, is turned towards optimism, regeneration and creation.

This is in stark contrast to the cynicism of Ouologuem in *Bound to Violence*. Hence, it is not fair to club them together in the same category as it has been done by Armah's compatriot, Kofi Awoonor. He remarks:

> The contemporary novel in Africa seems to be locked in an agonized search for a vision of political excellence on that continent. But this is merely a reflection of the social reali-

> ties of the politics of Africa. Perhaps the African novelist has not yet been able to break from the cycle of angst and frustration. The Malian novelist Yambo Ouologuem and the Ghanaian novelist Ayi Kwei Armah seem to epitomize this era of intense despair.[9]

A careful reading of Armah's works in general and *Two Thousand Seasons* in particular forcefully negates any such interpretations. Wole Soyinka, in this respect, betrays profound understanding of Armah's vision with particular reference to the present novel. He maintains thus:

> The actions of his protagonists are aimed at the retrieval of that past, but again Armah insists that this past is not a nostalgic one or sentimental one. It is presented as a state embodying a rational ideal. Armah goes even further; actions and motivations are deliberately contrived to place such longings (for a nostalgic past) in a context of betrayal of the larger aim; as self-delusion, self-destruction and general mindlessness. In the same way as the materialist retrogression of the modern African polity is an implied target of the author's savage attack, so also is the romanticism of Negritude assailed in associative portrayals.[10]

Armah's *Two Thousand Seasons* has humanism as its basic underlying ethic. The epic-dialectic form, directed towards the realization of a collective goal, makes the novel a milestone in African fiction. The scenes of transportation of the slaves, evoking mental and physical struggle against colonialism proper, are some of the most moving and poignant in the realm of English fiction. The dynamics of African history and society provides an encompassing vision in which the dialectics of social transformation demand an end to exploitation of all sorts. In his mission of pathfinding, Armah discovers beauty in reciprocity and connectedness and the beautiful ones in thinkers, healers and revolutionaries.

NOTES

1. Ayi Kwei Armah, *Two Thousand Seasons* (Nairobi: East African Publishing House, 1973; London: Heinemann Educational Books, 1979). All page references are to the Heinemann edition.
2. Bernth Lindfors, "Armah's Histories," *African Literature Today,* No. 11 (1980), p. 90.
3. Kirsten Holst Peterson, Review of the Novel entitled "The New Way," *WLWE*, Vol. 15, No. 2 (November 1976), p. 335.
4. Emmanuel Ngara, *Stylistic Criticism and the African Novel* (London: Heinemann, 1982), p. 142.
5. Hugh Webb, "The African Historical Novel and the Way Forward," *African Literature Today*, No. 11 (1980), p. 33.
6. Isidore Okpewho, "Myth and Modern Fiction: Armah's *Two Thousand Seasons,"* *African Literature Today,* No. 13 (1983), p. 3.
7. Rand Bishop, "The Beautyful Ones Are Born: Armah's First Five Novels," *WLWE*, Vol. 21, No. 3 (Autumn 1982), p. 532.
8. Ayi Kwei Armah, "African Socialism: Utopian or Scientific?" *Presence Africaine*, No. 64 (1967), p. 8.
9. Kofi Awoonor, *The Breast of the Earth* (New York: Double day, 1975), p. 304.
10. Wole Soyinka, *Myth, Literature and the African World* (Cambridge Univ. Press, 1976), pp. 112- 13.

The Beautiful Ones Are Born: *The Healers*

Armah's last novel to date, *The Healers*,[1] is a fictional representation of the social and revolutionary imperatives involved in the process of the liberation of the mind. The novel offers a microcosmic presentation of restorative processes providing a healing touch to the battered collective psyche. Like the earlier novels, it is aimed at self-assertion. The novel presents a culmination of conflicting values set on a course of imminent collision which, however, move in the direction of positive change, affirmation and resolution with a clean narrative supporting part-history and part-fiction.

If *Two Thousand Seasons* is characterized by thematic and structural polarities, *The Healers* offers a unison of theme and structure. In fact, the fragmented narrative of the earlier novels is replaced by a carefully ordered narrative with the novel divided into seven chapters and each chapter further divided into six parts with sub-titles providing a hint of the story-line. Although the novel is sub-titled as 'Historical Novel' it cannot be called authentic history for facts and figures do not form a part of the narrative and even the characters and events are out of place for a true historical novel.

The disintegration of the Asante empire during the last quarter of the nineteenth century due to an amalgam of factors—primarily because of the British aggression and lack of unity among the native tribes—provides the background against which Armah's fictional imagination transposes the healing community into a creative and regenerative force. It also provides the immediate context and necessary frame of reference for the exposition of the problem of good and evil which is central to Armah's fictional credo. The heroic struggle and the subsequent defeat of the Asante army against the invading British army forms an obscure part of history of the blacks which is transformed by Armah into a launching pad for analysing and examining the strengths and weaknesses of a group ethic from an historical point of view. According to Robert Fraser,

> The historical episode on which Armah chooses to concentrate is one which has been subject to a peculiar amount of misrepresentation by European historians. Seen from the Western point of view, the history of the late nineteenth century has often been seen as a process of rapid expansion of colonial frontiers, the bringing of the light to 'darkest Africa' being but a benign offshoot of this development. In this scenario, the final humiliation of a remote African people during the Second Asante War features as a minor, though piquant peccadillo, an obscure and often ignored sub-paragraph in school text-books.[2]

What Armah has in mind is the larger historical perspective which resolves the contradictions that govern the African polity and psyche. The obscure event as recorded in history is transformed into a viable paradigm for the historical processes that could have taken place anywhere in Africa not confined to a particular place. Armah's vigorous search for a catalyst of change is amply rewarded and his faith in the artist-figure vindicated with the healing community providing the much-needed impetus to the struggle against the stifling socio-political order.

The summation of conflicting values so brilliantly brought out in *Two Thousand Seasons* is once again in full display in this novel. The therapeutic value which the society is in need of is evocatively brought out in the title itself which, in fact, suggests the unifying force that binds the thematic and structural principles of the novel as well. The healing community could be traced back to the pre-colonial periods and Armah's attempt at finding a viable alternative takes him not merely to the historical recesses but to the precise point of history when the healing profession was treated with respect.

In Armah's fictional creation, the healers have a significant place in literal and symbolic sense. The thematic antecedents of the novel could be traced back to the prominence attributed to the healing profession in *Two Thousand Seasons* wherein Isanusi, the master healer, has shown 'the way' to the core members of the revolutionary group. The healers have a dual purpose in this context of social transformation. Their immediate concern is with the healing touch at the physical level and preparation of the natives for the long and arduous struggle at a purely psychological level. Their symbolic significance lies in their attempts to recapture and restore the pre-colonial system of a just and egalitarian social order. They look back to their roots and live in forests as a result of their refusal to become attached to and participate in the process of disintegration. The negation of the inviduous distinctions and moral bankruptcy has necessitated the re-creation of the cherished ideal. The healers are at once the representatives and harbingers of restorative processes set in the direction of a meaningful co-existence. The special symbolic significance attached to the healers and their therapeutic value truly brings out the core of the revolutionary imperative and the essence of the social change that Armah's visionary ideal projects. The restorative process of healing is slow and as practitioners of the art, the healers know it better. Damfo, the master-healer, tells Densu, the healer-initiate:

> There will be always work for healers, even when the highest work is done. That highest work, the bringing together again of the black people, will take centuries. (83)

The oral method of narration brilliantly serves the exposition of the group consciousness in the process of realizing the 'highest work.' The story-line is exposed by the story-teller in the beginning itself and the omniscient narrator is more eloquent and impressive than in *Two Thousand Seasons*:

> Is it a story of yesterday, or is it of last year? . . . Is it of that marvellous black time before the desert was turned desert, thirty centuries and more ago? Or have you let the listener know the truth: that this story now is not so old—just over a century old? (2-3)

The technique of a collective voice addressing itself to the audience, introduced early in *Two Thousand Seasons* is mastered in *The Healers* with consummate skill and perfection. Both the novels are thematically concerned with the African past and they sustain the ideological grip initially projected through the morbidity of the contemporary African society in the earlier three novels. Thus, the exposition of the collective consciousness through the communal voice and the oral tradition is at once a contrast and a complement to the all-pervading sense of betrayal and guilt as discernible in the first three novels. Robert Fraser, for instance, thinks that it is an important milestone in the annals of African fiction:

> . . . it can be stated without exaggeration that the development of the collective voice observable in the later books amounts to a revolution, not only in Armah's art in particular, but for the African novel in general.[3]

In keeping with the oral tradition, Armah makes an effective use of invocation, flashbacks and digression in the course of the narrative. The collective voice invokes the master of eloquence for words:

> Send me words, Mokopu Mofolo. Send me words of eloquence. Words are mere wind, but wind too has always been part of our work, this work of someone for the future, the work of story-tellers, the work of masters in the arts of eloquence. (52)

The problem of good and evil which is central to Armah's fictional credo and which underlines his moral vision is presented in this novel in the categorization of 'manipulators' and 'inspirers' representing opposing sets of values. The manipulators are those who intend to annex the freedom of the natives and initiate the process of colonization. The category also includes those native betrayers, the askari-zombis of *Two Thousand Seasons* whose nature is characterized by their self-centredness and willing servitude of the alien marauders. Ababio, the classic example of 'middleman,' Governer Glover, General Wolseley and the other generals of the British army are the 'manipulators' in the novel.

On the other, there are 'inspirers' whose vocation it is to awaken the people and participate in the processes of regeneration. These include Densu, the protagonist, Damfo, the master-healer, Asamoa Nkwanta, the General of the Asante army, Araba Jesiwa, the princess of Esuano and a host of healers who are all committed to the process of restoration. Out of this dialectic between the two conflicting attitudes the communal voice attempts to offer a positive note, a synthesis of past model and future course.

Densu is a personification of comprehensive vision, revolutionary ideology and militant action. In this respect, he embodies the non-corruptible vision of the anonymous man of *The Beautyful Ones Are Not Yet Born*, the ideological fervour of Baako in *Fragments*, and the revolutionary action of the militant group in *Two Thousand Seasons*. For Densu, communal welfare takes precedence over personal laurels and his story is a continuous search for such a social order. With a sound physique and sharp reflexes, he could have easily become the champion of the various games and eventually the king of Esuano. But he does not believe in individual glory that does not carry communal ethic with it.

The gulf between Densu and his immediate community is apparent in their reaction to the 'ceremonial games' which were elaborately described in the novel. These games, 'trials of individual strength and skill' degenerated into futile exercises with a single person being chosen as victor and isolated for the admiration of spectators and the envy of the defeated competitors. Once, these rituals had 'celebrated the struggles of a people working together to reach difficult destinations.' But now, the meaning of 'the ceremonies of unity had faded' (6). It was this gulf between the meaning of rituals in the past and present that had disturbed Densu even at the tender age of fourteen. His line of thinking substantiated by his choice of work later on, underlines the all-important sense of priorities in the enactment of personal and social drama:

> What sense was there in excluding the whole community from the centre of the field, leaving only a few grim battles? Why should everything have to end in a senseless victory for one isolated individual? What meaning could such a ritual give community turning as it did into a defeated mass, all

worshipping a lone victor? (39)

The novel could well be taken as an extension and a frame of reference for this conflict between a society that is deeply rooted in trivialities and a group of individuals who are out to redeem it by offering a healing touch.

II

Densu's entry into the healing profession is preceded by intense self-examination and meticulous analysis of the objective world which throws up a complex set of events such as intrigue, deceit, murder and escape. The internal situation is marked by his stiff resistance to the personality-oriented scenario and the cult of hero-worship. We get a glimpse of his character when he rejects the offer made by his childhood guardian, Ababio, to place himself 'on the right side of things as they come' (29). Densu's rejection of the offer is an expression of his moral choice that categorises him with other fictional protagonists of Armah. But unlike the man in *The Beautyful Ones Are Not Yet Born* and Modin in *Why Are We So Blest*?, he decides his choice of work on his own without ever becoming a passive witness to the disintegration of his cherished values. He not only preserves his integrity in the most adverse circumstances but reaches the interiors of the eastern forest to realize the ambition of becoming a healer himself.

Densu is not alone in his mission of path-finding. In the initial stages of his struggle at Esuano, he is closely associated with Anan who proves to be a true friend. Besides, there is Damfo and other healers whose empathy for Densu is matched only by their unstinted efforts to provide therapy to a society that is in a constant state of decline in terms of old systems, values and meaningful existence. Damfo realizes the potential of Densu very early and chooses him as a catalyst for social justice. Even as a child, Densu took a liking for the vocation of healers and constantly wished to be in the company of Damfo. He meets Damfo on one of his visits to Araba Jesiwa's house. The child's inquisitiveness apart, the dialogue between Densu and Damfo brings into sharp focus the sense of purpose on the part of the master-healer and the healer-initiate:

> 'Can anyone become a healer?'
> 'Few ever want to be healers.'
> 'But could everyone be a healer?'
> 'No.'
> 'Why not?'
> 'The healer must have a healing touch.'
> 'What is that?'
> 'I can't tell you what it is, just so,' said Damfo. But for a beginning he who would be a healer must see great value on seeing truly, hearing truly, understanding truly, and acting truly.' The healer laughed at himself. 'You see why healing can't be a popular vocation? The healer would rather see and hear and understand than have the power over men. Most people would rather have power over men than see and hear' (80-81).

The external situation also precipitates the decision of Densu to move into the eastern forest in search of Damfo. Ababio does not leave him alone and persists with his proposal of unlimited money and power if Densu agreed to serve the Britishers. Ababio encourages him to win the games so that the path would be cleared for his coronation as the king of Esuano in place of Appia, the heir-apparent, who had to win all the games to prove his merit:

> 'And don't let Appia worry you. Yes, he is the heir, but power doesn't always go to those who most expect it. Those who decide these things have been watching you. They know, for instance, what everybody knows: that you'll be the winner of these games, and these things are important; you have no idea just how important.'
> 'Do you mean the games have something to do with the holding of power at Esuano?' Densu asked, surprised.
> 'More than you think.' Ababio laughed, a totally relaxed laugh. 'Far more than you think. You'll see soon enough. After you win the games, many a surprise will be waiting for you, along whichever path you walk. All you have to do is to

be yourself, Densu, and win. I envy you' (38).

Densu knows that he is not cut out for such a personality cult. Instead, he visualises a society wherein 'there would be no competitors, only participants.' It was an ideal world in which the community members 'would be free to work together in the cool of the morning; they would be free to run, swim, jump, play, to celebrate health and strength in the late afternoon; they would dance to their own songs in the quiet of evenings' (39). In such a beautiful world, things would naturally be 'good.'

Densu subsequently shows little interest in water games and shooting competitions, having firmly decided on his choice of work. He does not even partake in the victory celebrations. He was glad that the game had come to an end, not only 'because he disliked the competitions themselves,' but also because 'his mind was powerfully drawn to something far from them.' It was also because 'he was eager to make the journey to the eastern forest.' He was eager to see the healer Damfo again, eager to talk to him about the future he had already chosen in his mind, a life spent devoted to the work of healing' (46). The most worried man at the decision of Densu was Ababio who chides him for throwing away what could have been a well-deserved victory for 'a natural-born victor.' He also warns Densu about the things in store for him if he does not toe his line:

> You know my secrets. A man who shares your secrets is your friend. There is no other thing he can possibly be—except your enemy. He works with you. Or he works against you. (47)

Ababio, true to his words, strikes very fast. The morning after the festival night marking prince Appia's victory in the games of youth, the prince was found murdered on a path leading from Esuano to the eastern forest. In the evil-design of Ababio, the elimination of Appia forms part of the strategy while pinning the needle of suspicion on Densu completes his game-plan. He does this with uncanny precision and skill. After Appia's burial, rumours were agog at Esuano that Ababio had a dream in which the dead prince's spirit promised him to help him find the way to the truth about his murder and about the disappearance of his mother,

Araba Jesiwa. Ababio himself was not to be found to confirm the rumours but his friend, Esuman, the court priest, does all the talking about the murder and counsels patience.

The death of Appia delays Densu's preparation for the journey to the eastern forest. But he could not remain at Esuano for 'the very air of Esuano had come for him charged with hostility and the slightest contact with it agitated his mind' (61). He could not postpone his visit any longer. On his way to the forest, he was flooded with memories of Ajoa, daughter of Damfo, his first meeting with Damfo, and Araba Jesiwa's aborted marriage.

Damfo advises restraint on Densu's part in his desire to become a healer and explains to him the seven rules which a learner had to scrupulously follow. He also advises him to go to Esuano to take leave of the near ones and spend one year there which would be the time of farewells:

In Densu's absence, Ababio creates an impression among the people of Esuano that Densu might be the culprit in the murder of Appia as the pieces of muscle from the dead prince's arms, his strong legs and also his eyes were stolen probably out of jealousy. Consequently, Densu was captured by a team headed by Ababio on his way to Esuano and was forcefully imprisoned in a house for the ensuing trial. When alone, Ababio himself confesses that he had arranged for the murder of Appia by the giant Buntui and he would certainly enjoy Densu's trial the next day. At the trial itself, Densu was the first person to be offered the poison-bark which would have killed him. Anan who has all along been guarding him pretending as one of the men of Ababio rescues him and both of them plunge into darkness. The people of Esuano chase them with the intention of capturing them dead or alive. Both of them try to escape to the eastern forest, but Anan dies on the way and Densu, himself severely injured, falls unconscious in the forest where Damfo picks him up. After his recovery, Densu sees Araba Jesiwa in one of the safe places in the forest, severly paralysed and without speech and consciousness.

The therapeutic value of the healing vocation is clearly brought out in the case histories of Araba Jesiwa and Asamoa Nkwanta. The treatment involved in the process of recovery is both physical and psychological. Araba Jesiwa was forced to marry Bedu Addo, a man hailing from an aristocratic family much against her wishes. Social customs come in the way of her marriage with a man of her choice. She remains childless for a long time with many miscarriages leading to frustration. She approaches Damfo for treatment who advises her to remove the artificial barriers in fulfilling her heart's desire. When she marries Kofi Entsua with whom she had fallen in love, she gives birth to a healthy male-child. But the murder of her son, Appia, to which she was a witness shocks her so much that she remains unconscious for a long time. Under the watchful eye of Damfo, she recovers slowly.

Asamoa Nkwanta's problems are purely psychological. In the wake of the death of an Asante king, one of the nephews of Nkwanta was offered as sacrifice. The gruesome killing makes Nkwanta reluctant to serve the Asante royals anymore having received the 'reward' for assiduously building up the Asante army. He comes to Praso seeking mental peace. The healers at Praso decide that Damfo would be the right choice for the job and send a word for him. Damfo sees the possibilities of nurturing Nkwanta into an instrument of a new social order. After the recovery of Densu in the eastern forest, the team of Damfo, Araba Jesiwa, Densu and Ajoa travel across the river Pra and reach Praso. The psychological therapy offered by Damfo had a soothing effect on the mind of Nkwanta:

> 'Have you thought of the future? The past steals energy from your soul because it forces you to think of a loss you're impotent to prevent. The future may bring you energy—if it can show you ways to work against that kind of loss' (178).

It is significant to note that the recovery of Araba Jesiwa and Asamoa Nkwanta was simultaneous bringing cheers to the healing community at Praso. Araba Jesiwa gradually regains her speech and shows marked improvement in her response to the treatment. Asamoa Nkwanta positively responds to the healing touch provided by Damfo to his bruised psyche. He tries to posit himself and his role in a larger perspective; in the interests of the native community, he decides to resume his duties as the General of the Asante army. With the immediate problem of the British invasion looming large, he decides to send Densu to Cape Coast to keep a watch on their strategies. Asamoa Nkwanta returns to Kumase where the Asante royals urge him to give the warriors 'the spirit they need' (240) and also lead the army against the impending assault by the white men. Asamoa Nkwanta agrees to it and spells out his strategy of detaining the white army in the forest as long as possible which they cannot withstand. Densu's splendid job of spying at Cape Coast is followed by his trip to Ada where another British General, Captain Glover, was making all out efforts to launch the attack on the Asante. He also collects the vital information of Glover receiving orders from Wolseley at Cape Coast and that they would be launching their attack in a month's time.

Asamoa Nkwanta remains unaware of the behind-the-door intrigues going on among the royals. According to the original plan, the net of the army would retreat as a trap for the white invaders bringing them deeper into the forest, where the warriors from Juaben, under Asafo Adjei, were expected to circle round behind the whites and bring up the end of the net. Due to the last minute changes in the strategy by the royals of which Asamoa Nkwanta was kept out, the whites march ahead without much resistance and the fall of the Asante inevitably follows.

After the defeat of the Asante army, Densu returns to Esuano to expose the crimes of Ababio, now the king of Esuano, and Esuman, the court priest. Ababio is rejoiced to see him and arranges a trial for Densu with a white judge. But the trial proves counterproductive as the dramatic appearance of Araba Jesiwa in the court-hall and her witness provides clinching evidence of the heinous crime of Ababio, Buntui and Esuman. The white judge frees Densu and sends the two culprits to Cape Coast for trial.

Although the novel reads like an adventure story, it is in keeping with the oral narrative in which the narrator is expected to celebrate the exploits of the hero with the specific purpose of enthusing his audience. Armah's fictional imagination transforms the oral method into a novelistic medium which attempts to convey a sense of justice, beauty, relationship and connectedness by means of healing touch and medicative processes. Besides, the supreme task of providing an alternative social order transcends what surfacially looks like a simple story-line into an all-important cleansing mechanism.

The resounding words of Ama Nkroma, the healer at Cape Coast, at the end of the novel sharply focus the resonant and comprehensive vision the novel so forcefully presents. During the victory celebrations of the whites, blacks from different countries and communities are brought to one place thus symbolically forging unity among the blacks. Ama Nkroma, with tears in her eyes, sees the possibilities of unity and healing touch even as the whites try to divide and rule them:

> 'It's a new dance all right,' she said, 'and it's grotesque. But look at all the black people the whites have brought here. Here we healers have been wondering about ways to bring our people together again. And the whites want ways to drive us farther apart. Does it not amuse you, that in their wish to drive us apart the whites are actually bringing us work for the future? Look!' (298)

The novel, exuding as such optimism and vitality, abounds in fertility motifs. The motif of feminine fertility and regeneration is conveyed through the process of Araba Jesiwa regaining strength and vigour and through Ajoa who is a symbol of pure love and inspiration. The tender love scenes of Ajoa and Densu further strengthen the fertility motif. Water forms an important motif in the novel as indeed all of Armah's protagonists are irresistibly drawn to water. What emerges from the following paragraph is life-sustaining principle merging the human with Nature:

> The world was warm. He felt a great need for water, water inside his body, water outside him, water covering him entirely. So he went to the nearest stream. He left his cloth on a rock overhanging the stream where it made a pool and plunged under the water. He closed his eyes and let his sense of direction go, not trying to hold on to anything. (230)

The motif of fertility is so predominant in the novel that even rivers are described in male and female terms. Nsu Ber, one of the two rivers that flowed by Esuano, was such a 'clear thing of beauty' (3) that people called it a female river. Its flow was so gentle that there were places 'where its moth motion was barely visible' whereas the second stream, Nsu Nyin, the male river, was heavy, turbulent and physically forceful. It is not merely water that provides an imagic pattern for regeneration but air, earth and forest converge on a natural sequence in providing a cyclic thrust to the process of healing.

The Healers offers a positive and integral vision which in many ways, is a continuation of Armah's reflections on the socio-historical realities in Africa. In his attempts to create a literary strategy in which dialectics and social dynamics play a significant role, Armah provides a summation of his ideological thrust in the novel. With its stress on fertility, creation, inspiration and regeneration the novel ultimately proves to be a culmination of Armah's fictional concerns, singular and variegated, dynamic and multi-dimensional in both analytical and constructive phases. Besides, the oral method of narration employed in the novel gives a new dimension to the art of fiction in English and coupled with its thematic concerns, the novel remains, like the healing vocation, a path-breaker and a path-finder.

NOTES

1. Ayi Kwei Armah, *The Healers* (Nairobi: East African Publishing House, 1978; London: Heinemann Educational Books, 1979). All page references are to the Heinemann edition.
2. Robert Fraser, *The Novels of Ayi Kwei Armah* (London: Heinemann, 1980), p. 85.
3. *Ibid.*

Conclusion

Armah's visionary construct is an articulation of his philosophy which from the beginning has been directed to the awakening of his people. It represents the concern of a young enthusiast and a creative artist for a better deal for the African, subjected to ruthless oppression and remorseless exploitation for a long time. It is informed by an awareness that the present disgrace is a spin-off of the man-made calamity of the colonialist and exploitative unnaturalness.

As it has been demonstrated so far, Armah's fictional frame in the analytical stage is marked by a diagnosis of the malady affecting the African society in general and the Ghanaian society in particular. It is followed by a positive and constructive sweep of African history and ideals in the second phase as part of an attempt to show the way out from the present morass. It has also been demonstrated that these two phases in Armah's fiction are complementary to each other. As such, his fiction becomes a manifestation of the dynamics of reciprocity and wholeness.

Armah is clearly on the side of the oppressed. His moral outrage at the 'dismemberment of things that could have made a whole'[1] is an outcome of his fervent concern for the vast exploited masses. Armah's vision, whatever expression it takes, is always focussed on the future of Africa. The diagnostic process of locating the genesis of the problem and the launching of a vigorous search for the lost way are only an expression of his vision of future and Pan-Africanism. The process of filtering the strengths from weaknesses of a collective predicament marks an imaginative flight into the recesses of African history as a preparatory exercise for the liberation of the mind. As Robert Fraser remarks, the supreme task of reconstruction results in 'a heightened form of the historical novel.'[2] In a dialectical and inspirational sweep, he reminds the people of their communal past without ever becoming racial or nostalgic.

Armah's secular vision is evidenced in the process of affirmation of the past whose social philosophy is natural egalitarianism. It also implies the unravelling of the factors responsible for the conflict with materialist set-up and outside cultures. In the process, he subjects the foreign invaders and the native cripples to a devastating criticism. Armah's fictional creation attains a unified vision by defining the way of wholeness and reciprocity and focussing the attention of the natives on the life-conserving energy inherent in them. With his Janus-like approach, Armah's depiction of the African reality has more far-reaching and wide-ranging dimensions than in any other African writer.

Much of African writing is distinguished by its educative quality. This aspect modifies the sensibility of the writer and decides the nature of the work of art in the African context. The donning of the role of a spokesman of a whole community is not uncommon in the realm of African letters. Achebe, for instance, emphasizes the educative function in writing:

> A writer who feels the need to right this wrong cannot escape the conclusion that the past needs to be created not only for the enlightenment of our detractors but even for our education. Because . . . the past with all its imperfections, never lacked dignity.[3]

In addition, Armah is basically a democratic artist. His realization of the role of an educator is part of his strategy as a writer. It includes the functions of a social scientist, curator, healer and a pathfinder.

The artist-saviour figure assumes centrality in Armah's fiction. His protagonists are drawn from and variously referred to as visionaries, seers, utterers, hearers and prophets. Their orientation is basically artistic and in their vocation they are committed to the cause of the exploited masses. They brood upon and participate in the process of social transformation. Despite the varied conditions of social upbringing, psychological make-up and different levels of participation in the constructive work, the thinking of the visionary protagonists is marked by a sense of duty 'to communicate with others, to influence, shape and guide individual as well as community life.'[4]

Armah's visionary-artist-intellectual protagonists provide a clue to Armah's literary ideology in the face of his stubborn refusal to give expression to his views in other than his fictional medium. Chidi Amuta rightly points out that Armah's fictional work can be approached from two different, but organically related positions of sociological criticism and theoretical poetics. This, according to Amuta, is possible

> First, because Armah is a manifestly committed artist who takes as his primary constituency the entire African continent and as his preoccupation the broad spectrum of Africa's experience since its contact with aliens (Westerners and Arabs), any consideration of his art and sensibility has wider implications. In this regard, to view his artist protagonists is to attempt a critique of his perception of the contemporary African artist and his social relevance. Secondly, because his artist characters are primarily fictional creations we are confronted with the problem of dealing with characters who aspire to a heroic stature while at the same time clinging to a fundamentally artistic sensibility. The first problem belongs to sociological criticism while the second raises issues in theoretical poetics.[5]

In *Why Are We So Blest?*, Solo makes a revolutionary statement on the social commitment of the African artist in the neo-colonial context:

> The western artist is blest with that atrophy of vision that can see beauty in deliberately broken-off pieces of a world sickened with oppression's ugliness. I hear the call of that art too. But in the world of my people the most important first act of creation, that rearrangement without which all attempts at creation are doomed to falseness, remains to be done. Europe hurled itself against us not for creation, but to

> destroy us, to use us for creating itself. America, a growth of Europe, now deepens that destruction. In this wreckage there is no creative art outside the destruction of the destroyers. In my people's world, revolution would be the only art, revolutionaries the only creatures. All else is part of Africa's destruction. (231)

The man in *The Beautyful Ones Are Not Yet Born*, is a sensitive observer and commentator. Naana and Baako are creators in their thinking and vocation. As a script writer, Baako tries to relate himself to the masses. But his aborted experiment at Ghanavision underlines the futility of his choice. His attempts at extricating himself from the society kill his artistic sensitivity. The authorial voice in *Two Thousand Seasons* as discernible in the Prologue is hardly distinguishable from the collective voice of 'we' and the voice of Isanusi. The fundis, utterers, and imaginers of the novel are engaged in the task of reconstruction which also underlines the inspirational aspect of Densu and Damfo in *The Healers*.

Armah, thus, attributes a special significance to intellectuals and artists in the process of restructuring. Whatever may be the vocation, their creation must realize the supreme duty—'to end the oppression of the African, to kill the European beasts of prey, to remake ourselves' as Solo so explicitly strikes at in *Why Are We So Blest?*

Armah's output to date is a practical demonstration of the fusion of art and ideology. His prose-style is consistent with his thought-processes. From a seemingly somnambulistic beginning in the opening pages of *The Beautyful Ones Are Not Yet Born*, it passes through a medley of devices and techniques to finally reach a crescendo in *Two Thousand Seasons* and *The Healers*.

Armah is one of those rarely gifted writers in whom social vision and artistic excellence have found a perfect fusion. He invests his prose with rhythmic melodies and musical intones. The zeal with which Armah approaches the reality endows his fictional writing with a sense of urgency. His aesthetic ideology and stylistic stances corroborate with authorial ideology. His prose, as a powerful weapon administers shock treatment in the beginning and the same is transformed into a soothing instrument gradually. It reaches new poetic heights of inspiration bordering on the oral narrative in *Two Thousand Seasons* and *The Healers.*

What underlines the tenor of each of Armah's novels is his ability to see 'clearly' as Baako does in *Fragments* and portray it in a suitable idiom. Realism is an integral part of African literature, whatever form it takes in expression. Emmanuel Ngara, while making a classification of different types of realism in African fiction, points out that in Achebe, we find 'critical realism,' and in Ngugi and Sembene Ousmane 'socialist realism.' Armah, according to Ngara, is concerned with 'metaphoric and mythic realism.'[6] Armah, in fact, defies strict classifications and/or combines within the corpus of his fiction all these aspects of realism. A brief note of comparison of the real concerns of the writers mentioned will bring into focus the radical view of aesthetic ideology enunciated by Armah.

Achebe provides a faithful account of the traditional Igbo society without glossing over its weaknesses in *Things Fall Apart* and *Arrow of God*. He points out how corruption creeps into the body politic of Africa under the European influence in *No Longer at Ease* and *A Man of the People* in moderate terms. Armah's stand against neo-colonialism and corruption cannot in any way be termed as moderate. It is decidedly radical and militant and the spirit of the same is expressed in uncompromising and unequivocal terms. The 'national and critical realism' as evidenced in the analysis of the contemporary situation in *The Beautyful Ones Are Not Yet Born* and *Fragments* is transformed to suit the shift of emphasis in the second phase. The visionary flight into the egalitarian ideal of communal well-being takes Armah into the realm of socialist art as observable in *Two Thousand Seasons.*

Even in this respect, Armah differs from the pronounced Marxist orientation of Ngugi and Sembene Ousmane. Ngugi's vision of future and Pan-Africanism is expressed in class terms. He says:

> A writer in African languages should reconnect themselves to the revolutionary traditions of an organised peasantry and working class in Africa in their struggle to defeat imperialism and create a higher system of democracy and socialism in al-

liance with all the other peoples of the world.[7]

Ngugi's *Petals of Blood* is decidedly anti-imperialist in tune with his ideological commitment to socialism in a Marxian sense. As Ngugi himself says, 'the Kenya peasantry is the real actor'[8] in the novel. It is informed by greater ideological clarity and force than he had displayed in his previous novels. In fact, his earlier novels, *Weep Not Child* and *The River Between* are often categorised with Achebe's earlier novels as classic examples of critical realism. The point of emphasis from critical realism to socialist art has much to do with ideological and political background. In Armah's case the shift is necessitated more as a part of strategy than ideological clarity or force. The artistic-authorial ideology has remained consistent but the expression takes a more explicit and direct form with a particular audience in mind.

Ousmane's masterpiece, *God's Bits of Wood* derives its strength from the fictionalization of the railway workers' strike which realizes that colonialism was primarily a system of economic exploitation. Like Armah's *Two Thousand Seasons,* Ousmane's novel presents a number of characters—God's bits of wood—who in their sheer 'diversity of material conditions, psychological states, views and alignments'[9] present the contradictory forces in the larger colonial confrontation. As in *Two Thousand Seasons*, dialectics governs the structural design of *God's Bits of Wood.*

In both the novels, the authorial ideology directs the dialectical movement of actions, reactions, contradictions, corroboratives and alternatives in an inspirational sweep with socialist ideals providing the basic ethic. The historical sweep of *Two Thousand Seasons*, on the other hand, makes an explicit statement of and a scathing attack on the dehumanizing aspect of racism as lethal weapon in the exploitative armoury of colonialism. Armah is of the view that the health of the black identity could be restored only in the form of anti-colonial struggles marking the unity of a race and a continent.

Armah's awareness of the African situation is shaped and governed by an empirical view of reality. His vision as discernible in his fiction is guided by a profound humanistic ethic of communal welfare. In his bold attempt to offer a new novelistic form and a fresh sensibility, Armah also provides a new vigour and impetus to African fiction. The summation of Armah's fictional creation is like a probing searchlight into the mechanics of social organization and a penetrating beam into the dynamics of social change.

NOTES

1. Ngugi wa Thiong'o, "From the Corridors of Silence," *The Weekend Guardian* (21-22 October 1989), p. 3.
2.. Robert Fraser, *The Novels of Ayi Kwei Armah* (London: Heinemann, 1980), p. 104.
3. Chinua Achebe, *African Writers on African Writing* (London: Heinemann, 1979), p. 205.
4. Ayo Mamadu, "Reflections in a Pool: Armah's Art on Artists and the Arts," *Research in African Literatures*, 16 (Winter 1985), p. 515.
5. Chidi Amuta, "Portraits of the Contemporary African Artist in Armah's Novels," *WLWE*, Vol. 21, No. 3 (Autumn 1982), p. 468.
6. Emmanuel Ngara, *Art and Ideology in the African Novel* (London: Heinemann, 1985), pp. 112-16.
7. Ngugi wa Thiong'o, *Decolonizing the Mind* (London: Heinemann, 1986), pp. 29-30.
8. Ngugi wa Thiong'o, *Writers in Politics* (London: Heinemann, 1981), p. 94.
9. Chidi Amuta, *The Theory of African Literature* (London: Zed Books, 1989), p. 140.

Bibliography

Primary Sources

Novels

The Beautyful Ones Are Not Yet Born. Boston: Houghton Mifflin, 1968; London: Heinemann Educational Books, 1969.

Fragments. Boston: Houghton Mifflin, 1970; London: Heinemann Educational Books, 1974; Nairobi: East African Publishing House, 1974.

Why Are We So Blest? New York: Doubleday, 1972; London: Heinemann Educational Books, 1974; Nairobi: East African Publishing House, 1974.

Two Thousand Seasons. Nairobi: East African Publishing House, 1973; London: Heinemann Educational Books, 1979.

The Healers. Nairobi: East African Publishing House, 1978; London: Heinemann Educational Books, 1979.

Short Stories

"Asemka," *Okyeame*, 3 (December 1966), pp. 28-32.

"Yaw Manu's Charm," *Atlantic Monthly* (May 1968), pp. 89-95.

"An African Fable," *Presence Africaine*, 68 (May 1968).

"The Offal Kind" *Harper's Magazine*, No. 1424 (January 1969), pp. 79-84.

"Half Way to Nirvana," *West Africa* (Sept. 24, 1984), pp. 147-48.

Poem

'Aftermath' in *Messages: Poems from Ghana*. London: Heinemann, 1970.

Political Theory

"African Socialism: Utopian or Scientific?" *Presence Africaine*, No. 64 (1967), pp. 6-30.

"A Mystification: African Independence Revalued," *Pan-African Journal*, 2, No. 2 (1969).

"Fanon: The Awakener," *Negro Digest*, 18 (October 1969).
"Masks and Marx: The Marxist Ethos vis-a-vis African Revolutionary Theory and Praxis," *Presence Africaine*, No. 131, 1984.

Criticism

"Larsony or Fiction as Criticism of Fiction," *Positive Review*, No. 1, 1978.

Secondary Sources

Books

Achebe, Chinua. *Things Fall Apart*. London: Heinemann, 1958.
______. *A Man of the People*. London: Heinemann, 1966.
______. *Morning Yet on Creation Day*. London: Heinemann, 1975.
Amuta, Chidi. *The Theory of African Literature*. London: Zed Books, 1989.
Awoonor, Kofi, *The Breast of the Earth*. New York: NOK, 1975.
Dathorne, O.R. *African Literature in the Twentieth Century*, Minneapolis: Univ. of Minnesota Press, 1974.
Davidson, Basil. *Which Way Africa*. Middlesex: Penguin Books, 1964.
Fanon, Frantz. *The Wretched of the Earth*. Middlesex: Penguin Books, 1965.
Fraser, Robert. *The Novels of Ayi Kwei Armah*. London: Heinemann, 1980.
Gikandi, Simon. *Reading the African Novel*. London: James Currey; Nairobi: Heinemann, 1987.
Griffiths, Gareth. *A Double Exile*. London: Marion Boyaras, 1978.
Israel, Jaochim. *Alienation: From Marx to Modern Sociology*. Boston: Allyn and Bacon, 1971.
Larson, Charles. *The Emergence of African Fiction*. London: Indiana Univ. Press, 1971.
Lawson, William. *The Western Scar: The Theme of the Been-to in West African Fiction*. Ohio: Ohio Univ. Press, 1982.
McEwan, Neil. *Africa and the Novel*. New Jersey: Humanities Press, 1984.
Narasimhaiah, C.D. and Emenyonu, Ernest N., eds. *African Literature Comes of Age*. Mysore: Dhvanyaloka, 1988.
Ngara, Emmanuel. *Stylistic Criticism and the African Novel*. London: Heinemann, 1982.
Ngugi wa Thiong'o. *Homecoming*. London: Heinemann, 1972.
Nkosi, Lewis. *Tasks and Masks*. Essex: Longman Group, 1981.
Obiechina, Emmanuel, *Culture, Tradition and Society in the West African Novel*. Cambridge: Cambridge Univ. Press, 1975.

Palmer, Eustace. *An Introduction of the African Novel.* London: Heinemann, 1972.

______. *The Growth of the African Novel.* London: Heinemann, 1979.

Soyinka, Wole. *The Interpreters.* London: Heinemann, 1970.

______. *Season of Anomy.* London: Heinemann, 1980.

______. *Myth, Literature and the African World.* Cambridge: Cambridge Univ. Press, 1976.

Taiwo, Oladele. *An Introduction to West African Literature.* England Thomas Nelson and Sons, 1967.

Wauthier, Claude. *The Literature and Thought of Modern Africa.* London: Heinemann, 1966.

Wright, Derek. *Ayi Kwei Armah's Africa: The Sources of His Fiction.* London: Hans Zell Publishers, 1989.

Zahar, Renate. *Frantz Fanon: Colonialism and Alienation.* New York: Monthly Review Press, 1974.

Articles

Achebe, Chinua. "The Truth of Fiction," *Literary Half-Yearly (July 1981), pp. 2-15.*

______. "The Novelist as Teacher," *African Writers on African Writing*, ed. G.D. Killam (London: Heinemann, 1973), pp. 1-4.

______. "Where Angels Fear to Tread," *African Writers on African Writing*, pp. 4-7.

______. "The Role of the Writer in a New Nation," *African Writers on African Writing*, pp. 7-13.

Adeyemi, N.A. "The Major Artistic Achievements of Armah in *The Beautyful Ones Are Not Yet Born*," *Shuttle*, 8 (1980), pp. 46-48.

Amizu, Kolu. "The Theme of Corruption in *A Man of the People* and *The Beautyful Ones Are Not Yet Born*," *Legacy*, Vol. 3, No. 2 (1977), pp. 18-23.

Amuta, Chidi. "Portraits of the Contemporary African Artist in Armah's Novels," *WLWE,* Vol. 21, No. 3 (Autumn 1982), pp. 467-76.

______. "History, Contemporary Reality and Social Vision in Ayi Kwei Armah's *Two Thousand Seasons*," *Journal of the Literary Society of Nigeria*, 1 (1981), pp. 40-51.

______. "Ayi Kwei Armah and the Mythopoesis of Mental Decolonization," *UFAHAMU*, Vol. 10, No. 3 (1981), pp. 44-56.

______. "The Revolutionary Imperative in the Contemporary African Novel: Ngugi's *Petals of Blood* and Armah's *The Healers*." *Commonwealth Novel in English*, Vol. 3, No. 2 (Fall 1990), pp. 130-42.

Anniah Gowda, H.H. "The Colonial Encounter: Achebe's Criticism,"

Literary Half-Yearly (July 1981), pp. 17-22.

Anyidoho, Kofi. "Historical Realism and the Visionary Ideal: Ayi Kwei Armah's *Two Thousand Seasons*," *UFAHAMU*, 11 (1981/82), pp. 108-30.

Bishop, Rand. "The Beautyful Ones Are Born: Armah's First Five Novels," *WLWE*, Vol. 21, No. 3 (Autumn 1982), pp. 531-37.

Booth, James. "*Why Are We So Blest?* And the Limits of Metaphor," *Journal of Commonwealth Literature*, Vol. 15, No. 1 (1980), pp. 50-64.

Britwum, Atta. "Hero-Worshipping in the African Novel," *Asemka*, 3 (1975), pp. 1-18.

Brydon, Diana. "The Myths that Write Us: Decolonizing the Mind," *Commonwealth: Essays and Studies*, 10 (1987), pp. 1-14.

Busia, Abena P.A. "Parasites and Prophets: The Use of Women in Ayi Kwei Armah's Novels," *Ngambika: Studies of Women in African Literature*, eds. Carole Boyce Davies and Anne Adam Graves (Trenton: Africa World, 1986), pp. 89-113.

Egudu, R.N. "Criticism of Modern African Literature: The Question of Evaluation" *WLWE*, Vol. 21, No. 1 (Spring 1982), pp. 54-66.

Evans, Jennu. "Woman of the Way: *Two Thousand Seasons*, Female Images and Black Identity," *ACCALS Bulletin*, VI, I (1982), pp. 17-26.

Folarin, Margaret, "An Additional Comment on Ayi Kwei Armah's *The Beautyful Ones Are Not Yet Born*," *African Literature Today*, Vol. 5 (1971), pp. 116-29.

Griffiths, Gareth. "Structure and Image in Kwei Armah's *The Beautyful Ones Are Not Yet Born*," *Ghanaian Literatures*, ed. Richard K. Priebe (London: Greenwood Press, 1988), pp. 225-40.

Goldie, Terry. "A Connection of Images: The Structure of Symbols in *The Beautyful Ones Are Not Yet Born*," *Kunapipi*, I, 1 (1979), pp. 94-107.

Indrasena Reddy, K. "Optimism in Ngugi's *Petals of Blood*," *Kakatiya Journal of English Studies*, Vol. VIII (1987-88), pp. 134-43.

Iyasere, Soloman Ogbede. "African Critics on African Literature: A Study in Misplaced Hostility," *African Literature Today*, No. 7 (1975), pp. 20-27.

Izebaye, D.S. "The State of Criticism in African Literature," *African Literature Today*, No. 7 (1975), pp. 1-19.

______. "Ayi Kwei Armah and the 'I' of the Beholder," *A Celebration of Black and African Writing*, ed. Bruce King and Kolawole Ogungbesan (Oxford Univ. Press, 1975), pp. 232-44.

______. "Time in the African Novel," *The Journal of Commonwealth Literature*, Vol. XVII, No. 1 (1982), pp. 74-89.

Johnson, Lemuel A. "The Middle Passage in African Literature: Wole Soyinka, Yambo Ouologuem, Ayi Kwei Armah," *African Literature Today*, 11 (1980), pp. 62-84.

Johnson, Joyce. "The Promethean Factor in Ayi Kwei Armah's *Fragments* and *Why Are We So Blest?*" *WLWE*, Vol. 21, No. 3 (Spring 1982), pp. 497-510.

Jones, Eldred Durosimi. "Ten Years of African Literature Today," *African Literature Today*, No. 10 (1979), pp. 1-6.

Kibera, L. "Pessimism and the African Novelist: Armah's *The Beautyful Ones Are Not Yet Born*," *The Journal of Commonwealth Literature*, Vol. XIV, No. 1 (1979), pp. 64-72.

Kunene, Mazisi. "Problems in African Literature," *Research in African Literatures*, Vol. 23, No. 1 (Spring 1992), pp. 27-44)

Lazarus, Neil. "Implications of Technique in Ayi Kwei Armah's *The Healers*," *Research in African Literatures*, Vol. 13, No. 4 (Winter 1982), pp. 488-98.

______. "Pessimism of the Intellect, Optimism of the Will: A Reading of Armah's *The Beautyful Ones Are Not Yet Born*," *Research in African Literatures*, Vol. 18, No. 2 (Summer 1987), pp. 137-75.

Lindfors, Bernth. "The Blind Man and the Elephant," *African Literature Today*, No. 7 (1975), pp. 53-64.

______. "Armah's Histories," *African Literature Today*, No. 11 (1980), pp. 85-96.

Lobb, Edward. "Armah's *Fragments* and the Vision of the Whole," *Ghanaian Literatures* (London: Greenwood Press, 1988), pp. 253-64.

Maiangwa, Yusufu. "The Duty of Violence in Yambo Ouologuem's *Bound to Violence*," *New West African Literature* (London: Heinemann, 1979), pp. 71-79.

Maja-Pearce, Adewale. "Just Another Sick Book: On Ayi kwei Armah's *Why Are We So Blest?*" *Okike*, XXIII (1983), pp. 133-36.

Mallikarjuna Rao, P. "No Longer At Ease: A Note on African Writing," *Kakatiya Journal of English Studies*, Vol. VII (1987), pp. 73-81.

Mamadu, Ayo. "Reflections in a Pool: Armah's Art on Artists and the Arts," *Research in African Literatures*, Vol. 16, No. 4 (Winter 1985), pp. 514-24.

______. "Making Despair Bearable: Armah's *The Beautyful Ones Are Not Yet Born* and *Fragments*," *Neohelicon*, Vol. X, No. 2 (1983), pp. 231-49.

Massa, Daniel. "The Postcolonial Dream," *WLWE*, Vol. XX, No. 1, pp. 135-49. (Discusses *Fragments*).

Ngugi wa Thiong'o. "The African Writer and his Past," *Perspectives on African Literature*, ed. Christopher Heywood (London: Heinemann,

1971), pp. 3-8.

______. "From the Corridors of Silence" *The Weekend Guardian* (21-22 October 1989), pp. 2-5.

Nkosi, Lewis, "Individualism and Social Commitment," *The Writer in Modern Africa* (A collection of papers read at African-Scandinavian Conference, Stockholm, 1967) (New York: African Publication Corporation, 1969), pp. 45-51.

Nnolim, Charles, E. "Dialectic as Form: Pejorism in the Novels of Armah," *African Literature Today*, No. 10 (1979), pp. 207-23.

Nwahunanya, Chinyere. "A Vision of the Ideal: Armah's *Two Thousand Seasons*," *Modern Fiction Studies*, Vol. 37, No. 3 (Autumn 1991), pp. 549-66.

Obiechina, E.N. "Cultural Nationalism in Modern African Creative Literature," *African Literature Today*, No. 1 (1969), pp. 24-35.

Ogede, Ode S. "Armah in Americans: Identity Crisis in *Why Are We So Blest?*" *ARIEL*, 21 (1990), pp. 49-66.

______. "Two Decades of Armah Criticism (1968-1988): Trends, Achievements, Blind Spots," *Zast*, 7/8 (1990), pp. 41-53.

______. "Pattern of Decadence, Visions of Regeneration in Armah's *Fragments*," *Modern Fiction Studies*, Vol. 37, No. 3 (Autumn, 1991), pp. 529-48.

Ogungbesan, Kolawole. "Symbol and Meaning in *The Beautyful Ones Are Not Yet Born*," *African Literature Today*, No. 7 (1975), pp. 93-110.

Okonkwo, J.I. "Cultural Revolution and the African Novel," *UFAHAMU*, Vol. XIV, No. 3 (1985), pp. 103-13.

______. "The Missing Link in African Literature," *African Literature Today*, No. 10 (1979), pp. 86-105.

Okpewho, Isidore. "Myth and Modern Fiction," Armah's *Two Thousand Seasons*," *African Literature Today*, No. 13 (1983), pp. 1-23.

Ola, V.U. "The Feminine Principle and the Search for Wholeness in *The Healers*," *UFAHAMU*, Vol. XIV, No. 3 (1985), pp. 73-83.

Otu, Ato Sekyi. "Toward Anona . . . Not Back to Anoa: The Grammar of Revolutionary Homecoming in *Two Thousand Seasons*," *Research in African Literatures*, Vol. 18, No. 2 (Summer 1987), pp. 192-214.

Owomoyela, Oyekan, "Socialist Realism or African Realism? A Choice of Ancestors," *Research in African Literatures*, Vol. 22, No. 2 (1991), pp. 21-40.

Palmer, Eustace. "Negritude Rediscovered: A Reading of the Recent Novels of Armah, Ngugi and Soyinka," *International Fiction Review*, Vol. VIII, No. 1, pp. 1-11.

Peck, Richard. "Hermits and Saviors, Osagyefos and Healers: Artists and Intellectuals in the Works of Ngugi and Armah," *Research in Afri-*

can Literatures, Vol. 20, No. 1 (Spring 1989), pp. 26-41.

Peterson, Kirsten H. "Loss and Frustration: An Analysis of A.K. Armah's *Fragments*," *Kunapipi*, I, 1 (1979), pp. 53-65.

Ravenscroft, Arthur. "African Literature: Novels of Disillusion," *The Journal of Commonwealth Literature*, No. 6 (Jan. 1969), pp. 120-37.

Sackey, Edward. "Oral Tradition and the African Novel," *Modern Fiction Studies*, Vol. 37, No. 3 (Autumn 1991), pp. 389-407.

Simonse, Simon. "African Literature between Nostalgia and Utopia: African Novels since 1953 in the light of the Modes-of-production Approach," *Research in African Literatures*, 13, No. 4 (Winter 1982), pp. 452-87.

Soyinka, Wole. "Cross-Currents: The New African After Cultural Encounters," *Writers in East-West Encounter: New Cultural Bearings*, ed. Guy Amrithanayagam (London: Macmillan Press, 1982), pp. 51-63.

Taban lo Liyong. "Ayi Kwei Armah in Two Moods," *Journal of Commonwealth Literature*, Vol. XXVI, No. 1 (1991), pp. 1-18.

Utidjian, Eliane Saint-Andre. "Aspects of Myth in Two Ghanaian Novels," *Commonwealth: Essays and Studies*, 10 (1987), pp. 22-25.

Wright, Derek. "The Early Writings of Ayi Kwei Armah," *Research in African Literatures*, 16, No. 4 (Winter 1985), pp. 487-513.

______. "Orality in the African Historical Novel: Yambo Ouologuem's *Bound to Violence* and Ayi Kwei Armah's *Two Thousand Seasons*," *The Journal of Commonwealth Literature*, Vol. 23, No. 1 (1988), pp. 91-101.

______. "Saviours and Survivors: The Disappearing Community in the Novels of Ayi Kwei Armah," *UFAHAMU*, Vol. XIV, No. 2 (1985), pp. 134-56.

______. "The Metaphysical and Material Worlds—Ayi Kwei Armah's Ritual Cycle," *World Literature Today*, Vol. 59, No. 3 (Summer 1985), pp. 337-42.

______. "*Fragments*: The Akan Background," *Research in African Literatures*, Vol. 18, No. 2 (Summer 1987), pp. 176-91.

______. "Safety in Numbers: A Note on Numerology in African Writing," *The Literary Criterion*, Vol. XXVI, No. 3 (1991), pp. 31-37.

Webb, Hugh. "The African Historical Novel and the Way Forward," *African Literature Today*, 11 (1980), pp. 24-38.

Yeebo, Zaya. "Ghana: Defence Committees and the Class Struggle," *Review of African Political Economy*, No. 32 (April 1985), pp. 64-72.

Reviews

Jones, Eldred Durosimi. "Ayi Kwei Armah: *The Beautyful Ones Are Not Yet Born*," *African Literature Today*, No. 3, pp. 55-56.

Kisogie, B. "A Plague on Both your Houses," *Transition*, 45 (1973), p. 75; review of *Two Thousand Seasons*.

Lurie, J. "Fragments between the Loved Ones and the Community," *Bashiru*, Vol. V, No. 1 (1973), pp. 31-41.

Moore, Gerald. "Armah's Second Novel," *The Journal of Commonwealth Literature*, Vol. IX, No. 1 (August 1974), pp. 69-71.

Omotoso, Kole. "Mere Mirrors of Annihilation," *Afriscope*, IV, 7 (1973), pp. 42-43 (review of Soyinka's *Season of Anomy* and Armah's *Two Thousand Seasons*):

Thomas, P. "*Why Are We So Blest?* A Review," *African Arts*, Vol. VI, No. 3 (1973), pp. 81-82.

Yankson, Kofi. "*Fragments*: The Eagle that Refused to Soar," *Asemka*, I, 1 (1974), pp. 57-59.

Interviews

Achebe, Chinua. In interview with Kalu Ogbaa, *Research in African Literatures*, Vol. 12, No. 1 (Spring 1981), pp. 1-13.

Ngugi wa Thiong'o. "The Commitment of the Intellectual," in interview with Obi Bini, *Review of African Political Economy*, No. 32 (April 1985), p. 19.

Index

Achebe, Chinua 16, 17, 19-20, 22, 24, 30n, 31n, 33, 35, 53n, 54n, 125, 127n
"African Socialism: Utopian or Scientific?" 54n, 92, 107n
Arrow of God 19, 125
Awoonor, Kofi 21, 106, 107n

Beautyful Ones Are Not Yet Born, The 7, 8, 11, 12, 22, 23, 24, 26, 28-29, **33-54**, 55, 56, 61, 69, 74, 76, 79, 91, 107n, 112, 113, 124, 125
"Black Skin, White Masks" 36, 88n
Bound to Violence 106
Breast of the Earth, The 107n

Dante 34

Facing Mount Kenya 17, 30n
Fanon, Frantz 7, 8, 14, 15, 16, 30n, 31n, 36, 54n, 74, 85, 88n
Fragments 7, 11, 12, 22, 23, 24, 25, 26, 28, 29, **55-73**, 74, 77, 79, 85, 91, 112, 125

God's Bits of Wood 20, 126
Grain of Wheat, A 20, 21, 31n

Healers, The 7, 8, 11, 20, 22, 25, 28, 29-30, 73n, 74, **108-20**, 124, 125

Interpreters, The 22

Kenyatta, Zomo 17, 30n

Man of the People, A 22, 125
Morning Yet on Creation Day 53n

Ngugi wa Thiong'o 16, 19, 20, 30n, 72, 125, 126, 127n
No Longer at Ease 125

Oulouguem, Yambo 21, 26, 106
Ousmane, Sembene 20, 125, 126

Petals of Blood 126
Portrait of the Artist as a Young Man, A 25

River Between, The 126

Soyinka, Wole 21, 22, 26, 27, 31n, 54n, 107n
Swift, Jonathan 34

Things Fall Apart 19, 125
Two Thousand Seasons 7, 8, 11, 12-13, 20, 22, 24, 25, 27, 28, 29, 43, 69, 73n, 74, **89-107**, 108, 109, 110, 111, 112, 124, 125, 126

Weep Not Child 126
Why Are We So Blest? 8, 11, 12, 22, 23, 24, 28, 29, **74-88**, 91, 113, 123, 124
Wretched of the Earth, The 8n, 15, 30n, 54n, 88n, 91